LOW OR NO
TUITION

The Feasibility of a
National Policy for the
First Two Years of College

A PUBLICATION OF THE CARNEGIE COUNCIL
ON POLICY STUDIES IN HIGHER EDUCATION

*An Analytical Report
by the Carnegie Council
on Policy Studies
in Higher Education*

LOW OR NO TUITION

The Feasibility of a National Policy
for the First Two Years of College

Jossey-Bass Publishers
San Francisco • Washington • London • 1975

LOW OR NO TUITION
The Feasibility of a National Policy for the First Two Years of College
The Carnegie Council on Policy Studies in Higher Education

*This report is issued by the Carnegie Council on Policy Studies
in Higher Education with headquarters at 2150 Shattuck Avenue,
Berkeley, California 94704.*

*Copies are available from Jossey-Bass, San Francisco,
for the United States, Canada, and Possessions.
Copies for the rest of the world are available from
Jossey-Bass, London.*

Library of Congress Catalogue Card Number LC 75-4276

International Standard Book Number ISBN 0-87589-257-4

Manufactured in the United States of America

DESIGN BY WILLI BAUM

FIRST EDITION

Code 7508

Contents

Preface

As a contribution to the current discussion and debate over tuition policy in postsecondary education, the Carnegie Council has undertaken an analysis of the feasibility of achieving a national pattern of low or no tuition in the first two years of postsecondary education. One factor in our decision to undertake the study was the interest in such a project expressed by Stephen K. Bailey, vice-president, American Council on Education (ACE). Staff members of the ACE Policy Analysis Service have been kept informed of progress on the study at all stages.

We wish to express our appreciation for the helpful comments and suggestions of the persons who attended meetings held in Berkeley in October 1974 and in Washington, D.C., in November 1974 to discuss earlier drafts of the report. They included Robert Andringa, minority staff director, Committee on Education and Labor, U.S. House of Representatives; Kevin Bacon, University of California Student Lobby, Sacramento; Stephen K. Bailey, vice-president, ACE; George F. Break, professor of economics, University of California, Berkeley; John E. Coons, professor of law, University of California, Berkeley; André Danière, associate research professor of economics, Boston College; Miles Fisher, executive secretary, National Association for Equal Opportunity in Higher Education; Bruce Fuller, consultant, Joint Committee on Postsecondary Education, California State Legislature; Robert Hartman, senior fellow, The Brookings Institution; Engin Holmstrom, policy associate, ACE; John F. Hughes, director, Policy Analysis Service, ACE; Aims

McGuinness, Jr., executive assistant to the chancellor, University of Maine; Roy Radner, professor of economics, University of California, Berkeley; Jerold Roschwald, director, Office of Governmental Relations, National Association of State Universities and Land-Grant Colleges; Patricia Smith, policy associate, ACE; Allan Sindler, professor of public policy, University of California, Berkeley; Jay Stampen, senior policy associate, American Association of State Colleges and Universities; Martin Trow, professor of public policy, University of California, Berkeley; Carol Van Alstyne, chief economist, ACE; and Kenneth Young, director, American College Testing Program, Washington, D.C.

The Council also wishes to thank its staff members, and especially Margaret S. Gordon, for their work on this report.

William G. Bowen
President
Princeton University

Ernest L. Boyer
Chancellor
State University of New York

Nolen Ellison
President
Cuyahoga Community College

E. K. Fretwell, Jr.
President
State University of New York College at Buffalo

Rosemary Park
Professor of Education
University of California, Los Angeles

James A. Perkins
Chairman of the Board
International Council for Educational Development

Alan Pifer, *ex officio*
President
The Carnegie Foundation for the Advancement of Teaching

Lois Rice
Vice-President
College Entrance Examination Board

Pauline Tompkins
President
Cedar Crest College

Clifton R. Wharton, Jr.
President
Michigan State University

William Van Alstyne
Professor of Law
Duke University

Clark Kerr
Chairman
Carnegie Council on Policy Studies in Higher Education

1

Purpose
and Background

In 1947 the Zook Commission proposed that "tuition-free education should be available in public institutions to all youth for the freshman and sophomore years or for the traditional 2-year junior college course" (The President's Commission, 1947, vol. 1, p. 37). The Carnegie Commission, on several occasions, supported low or no tuition for public two-year colleges, and relatively low tuition for lower-division students in four-year institutions.[1] Renewed interest in such possibilities has recently been expressed by congressional leaders and within the higher education community.

This report by the Carnegie Council examines the feasibility of a national pattern of low or no tuition for the first two years of college. It is concerned primarily with two questions:

1. On the basis of an analysis of tuition policy and other closely related financing policies in the 50 states, what is the likelihood of concerted state action toward low or no tuition in the first two years of college?
2. Should the federal government become directly involved in encouraging low or no tuition policies in the first two years of postsecondary education through a new program of grants either to institutions or to states to achieve this objective?

[1] See Appendix.

The analysis is based on the premise that these questions cannot be seriously examined without a careful study of the factors associated with interstate variations in tuition charges in public institutions. On the basis of the results of this analysis, we conclude that:

1. Achievement of a national pattern of low or no tuition in the first two years of college through state action alone is improbable, in view of the trend toward rising tuition in public colleges and universities in many of the states and the growing emphasis on scholarship programs as a means of alleviating the effects of the rising tuition gap between public and private institutions.
2. Achievement of such a pattern through federal action would be most difficult, given the widely differing circumstances among the 50 states.
3. Tuition policy, for this and other reasons, is better subject to state and institutional action, as it has been historically, than to action by the federal government.
4. The federal government, in any event, should give its highest priority to those programs to which it is already committed and which are inadequately funded, and, in some cases, are inadequately developed. The Council's recommendations for federal policy in relation to postsecondary education have been included in its recent report, *The Federal Role in Postsecondary Education.*

The concept of "two years of free access" to higher education in the United States has a long history, dating back to some of the first public junior colleges established in the early years of the present century. The spread of the public junior college movement to practically all of the 50 states, the gradual development of the comprehensive community college to replace the older notion of a junior college, and the enormously rapid growth of enrollment in these public two-year institutions all testify to the increasing popularity of colleges that are geographically accessible, easy to enter, and relatively low cost.

As James B. Conant expressed it:

The extension of the years of free education through the establishment of local two-year colleges has been the expression of a new social policy of the nation. Or perhaps I should say a further thrust of an old policy. For one could simplify the history of American public education in the last hundred years by noting the steps in the movement to make universal opportunities hitherto open only to the well-to-do. First came the provision of elementary schools at public expense; then came the free high schools and efforts to provide instruction for a wide variety of talents (the widely comprehensive four-year high school); lastly, the growth of the equally comprehensive public two-year college, the open-door college, as it has been sometimes called (Conant, 1970, p. 637).

We must not forget, also, that most state universities and land-grant colleges have had a long tradition of very low or no tuition, from which some of them have departed only in relatively recent years. But these policies were designed to provide easily accessible and low-cost education throughout four undergraduate years and on into postbaccalaureate study—they were not especially associated with the concept of two years of free access. And in recent years tuition increases at four-year public institutions have become frequent, in the face of rising costs.

Also influential in accounting for the growing support for two years of free public education beyond the high school was the impact of technological development in increasing the demand for employees with paraprofessional training in a variety of fields, such as engineering and health technology, as well as business administration and office procedures. Increasingly, in an advanced industrial society, many high school graduates were not well equipped to meet the changing occupational requirements they would face as adults. And, if this was true of high school graduates, it was even more true of those who had dropped out before completing high school. Moreover, many of the most rapidly expanding employment opportunities were in occupations for which the community colleges could provide training, such as the allied health professions. The most recent addition to the list of occupations in which paraprofessional training is being provided is the field of law.

Supporters of low or no tuition in the first two years of college also have in mind some more general considerations relating to opportunity in postsecondary education. Many lower-division students, it is felt, are uncertain about their probability of succeeding and, sometimes, even of their motivation or taste for advanced study. They should be given maximum opportunity to try out their chances for successful achievement in postsecondary education in the first two years, with a minimal financial burden. Once a student has successfully advanced to upper-division work, he can be expected to be more confident and, if he wishes to continue in, or transfer to, an institution with costs beyond those available to him through student grants or his parents' contributions, should be prepared to augment his resources through part-time work or borrowing.

Policies of low or no tuition in the first two years of public postsecondary education also have great appeal to those who are especially concerned with encouraging educational opportunities for adults. Many of the students who enroll in low-cost public institutions, and especially in community colleges, are adults wishing to study on a part-time basis or to "come back to school" after some years in employment or, for married women, in household and child-rearing responsibilities. For many of these people, and especially for many married women, student aid under existing policies is not likely to be available, but low or no tuition may mean all the difference in making the option to enroll feasible.

It is important to keep in mind, however, that low tuition policies do not necessarily make it possible for young people from low-income families to enroll in nearby colleges. The problem of meeting subsistence costs and of incidental educational expenses, such as the cost of books, may make it impossible for them to attend in spite of low tuition and easy admissions policies. Thus, low-income youth are likely to need student aid even when low-cost colleges are accessible. In fact, some of them may not be in a position to attend even then, because their families cannot afford to get along without the earnings they might receive if not enrolled. Another way of putting this point is that "forgone earnings" represent a more serious sacrifice in relation to family income for young people from low-income families than for those from middle- and upper-income families.

There is, of course, a significant school of thought that opposes the entire concept of low tuition in public colleges and universities. Tuition in public institutions, a number of spokesmen for this position argue, should be raised to cover total educational costs, so that public subsidies can be more effectively targeted to needy students, and public and private institutions can compete for students and resources on a more even basis.[2] However, proposals to implement this principle, such as the Hansen-Weisbrod proposal in Wisconsin, have not gained much public support (Hansen and Weisbrod, 1970). Low tuition has strong popular appeal, and, also, there are many economists who, while appreciating the arguments of those who favor full-cost tuition, nevertheless believe that implementation of such a policy would force many young people to borrow heavily to achieve their degrees. It would, in effect, represent a sudden and perhaps unfair shift away from the more traditional pattern in which the parental generation has financed the education of the college generation, either through taxes or direct parental support.

The difficulties of maintaining low tuition in postsecondary education have been exacerbated in the last few years by accelerated inflation, which has frequently made it impossible for institutions to meet rising costs without substantial tuition increases. These accelerated tuition increases, in both public and private institutions, have played a role in stimulating renewed interest in a possible federal government policy designed to assist the states in maintaining low tuition in public postsecondary education.

[2] For a particularly effective statement of this point of view, see Nerlove (1972).

2

Public Two-Year Colleges

A relatively modest objective of proponents of low or no tuition in the first two years of postsecondary education might be to implement such a policy in public two-year colleges. Although there are rather substantial variations in tuition charges of these institutions from state to state, and even within states, average tuition and required fees are almost invariably lower in public two-year colleges than in public four-year institutions and much lower than in private colleges. Thus, the cost per FTE student of moving toward very low or no tuition in these colleges would be smaller than in four-year institutions. Moreover, there is widespread acceptance of the idea that public two-year colleges should pursue open-door policies, both with respect to tuition and to standards of admission.

Variations in Charges Within States

There are many pitfalls for the unwary in the use of statistics relating to tuition and required fees. For purposes of analysis of variations in the charges of public two-year colleges, we have used the data in the annual *Directory* of the American Association of Community and Junior Colleges (AACJC), but have had to make some adjustments in these statistics.[1]

[1] In some cases the reported charge was apparently for a quarter, rather than for a full year, in other cases comparison with data from other sources indicated that required fees were not fully reported.

Recently the U.S. National Center for Educational Statistics began to

Why should there be such wide variations in the charges of public two-year colleges within states, as well as among states, as indicated in Table 1? The answer lies chiefly in the fact that in a number of states the actual decisions about tuition and required fees, and especially the latter, are made by local rather than by state boards. For this reason we have indicated in the bottom row of Table 1 whether control is exercised entirely by a state board (*S*), or by both a state board and local boards (*S&L*), or in a mixed situation in which parts of the system (usually two-year branch campuses of four-year institutions) are under state control, while other parts (usually community colleges) are under state and local control (*M*). With the two-year branch campuses, state control usually means control by the board of trustees that controls the parent institution.[2]

---

report tuition and required fees in its annual directory of institutions of higher education, but the data are not always satisfactory for public two-year colleges, because the charges reported are those for state residents. In many of the states, there are actually three sets of charges in public two-year colleges—the lowest for residents of the local community college district, an intermediate charge for state residents who are not residents of the district, and a maximum charge for out-of-state students. Because the great majority of students in public two-year colleges tend to be residents of the district, it is the charge applicable to district residents that is of primary interest. This problem does not arise in the case of public four-year institutions, which have only two sets of charges, one for state residents and a higher set of charges for students who do not qualify as state residents.

The College Entrance Examination Board also reports student charges in its annual report entitled *Student Expenses at Postsecondary Institutions*, but the number of two-year public colleges included is very much smaller than in the case of the AACJC *Directory*.

[2]This classification is not intended to indicate whether state boards are governing boards or have only coordinating responsibilities. The situation varies considerably from state to state in this respect. Moreover, some states have separate boards for community colleges, while in others community colleges are under the jurisdiction of a broader board for all public institutions of higher education or a state board of education (Wattenbarger and Sakaguchi, 1971). The classification used here is intended only to indicate whether there are local boards of trustees that have some degree of decision-making power. It largely coincides with the classification of enrollment by control used by National Center for Educational Statistics in, for example, Table 84 in U.S. National Center for Educational Statistics (1973).

These differences in control are related to differences in sources of financing. Public two-year colleges in *S* states do not receive any of their funds from local sources, whereas some of those in *M* states and most of those in *S&L* states do receive some of their funds from local sources. Exceptions, among *S&L* states, are Florida, Georgia, and Washington, in which there are local district boards but little or no financing from local sources. In those states in which local tax funds provide part of the revenue of public two-year colleges, the proportion of revenue from this source varies widely.[3]

In general, there is a tendency for tuition and required fees in public two-year colleges to vary more widely in *S&L* and in *M* states than in *S* states. In *M* states, charges at two-year branch campuses are likely to be higher than at other public two-year colleges, usually equaling or falling only slightly below those of parent institutions. In *S&L* states, the widest variations are found in Illinois and New York, reflecting, in part, the fact that community colleges in Chicago and in New York City have no tuition, while those in other community college districts of these states have rather widely varying charges.[4] California community colleges have a long-standing policy, governed by state law, of charging no tuition for state residents, although a few of the colleges have begun to impose fees for such purposes as health services and parking.[5] Arizona also has a long-standing tradition of no tuition for district residents, while in Wisconsin the two-year technical institutes have no tuition and very modest fees. Apart from the three states of Arizona, California, and Wisconsin, and the cities of Chicago and New York, zero tuition is found in only a few scattered institutions.

Interstate Variations

Although there are substantial variations among states in tuition and required fees of public two-year colleges, charges continue to be comparatively low in most of the states. The overall

[3]See the table in National Commission on the Financing of Postsecondary Education (1973), pp. 395-396.

[4]Community colleges in New York City do, however, have tuition charges for part-time and evening students.

[5]In California and in a number of other states, community college districts

United States average, based on our analysis of AACJC data, was $252 in 1972-73.[6] One-sixth of the institutions had zero tuition, and another 65 percent had tuition and required fees of less than $400. Thus, the proportion of public two-year colleges with tuition and required fees of $400 or more was less than one-fifth of the total.

Statewide average charges varied from a low of $2 in California to a high of $860 in Vermont, while the charges of individual institutions varied from zero to more than $1,000.[7] In order to develop a proposal designed to implement a national policy of low or no tuition in public two-year colleges, it is necessary to analyze the factors associated with variations from state to state.

In our search for these factors, we have explored the following hypotheses:

1. Variations are related to differences in proportions of operating revenue received from local sources.
2. Variations are related to differences in per capita personal income among the states.
3. Variations are related to differences in the relative proportions of total state enrollment in private and public institutions.
4. Variations follow a regional pattern.
5. Variations are related to expenditures per student on state scholarship programs.

---

are reimbursed for their share of the educational costs of students attending from other districts within the state.

[6]This is an institutional average and is not weighted by enrollment. Weighting by institutions seems appropriate for our purposes, because we are interested in the structure of tuition charges. Weighting by enrollment would yield a measure dominated by the charges of the very large two-year colleges, which tend to be in large urban communities.

[7]The unusually high tuition charges of the two public two-year institutions in Vermont are explained by two factors: (1) a tradition of high tuition in public institutions in a state that has had difficulty in providing substantial funds for the development of public higher education and (2) the fact that there is no real system of public higher education in Vermont and that the state has no plans for development of a public community college system, comparable to those of most other states (letter from George V. Kidder, executive secretary, Vermont Higher Education Council, dated January 3, 1975).

The results of this analysis are presented in Tables 2 through 5 and in Table 16.

Among our hypotheses, only the first yielded no significant result. There was no consistent relationship between average tuition and required fees and the percentage of revenue received from local sources.

Average tuition and required fees did tend to rise with increasing per capita personal income among the states, but the relationship was not altogether consistent and, in fact, was reversed for states with per capita income of $5,000 or more. The main reason for this reversal is that several of the states with per capita income of $5,000 or more in 1972 are in the Pacific region, where there is a strong tradition of low-cost public higher education.

The finding that state differences in average charges of public two-year colleges are positively related to per capita income is, of course, consistent with the fact that, historically, nationwide average tuition has tended to rise at more or less the same rate as per capita income, at least in the long run.[8] Both tendencies reflect the fact that student charges at colleges and universities are strongly influenced by student ability to pay, and this is true even for many of the heavily subsidized public two-year colleges.

More consistent results are found when we examine the relationship between average tuition and required fees and the percentage of total state enrollment in private institutions. There are two main reasons for expecting a positive relationship between these two variables. In the first place, we might expect to find a strong tradition of low tuition in public higher education in states in which public institutions have been historically predominant. Second, where a substantial percentage of total state enrollment is in private institutions, we might expect the private institutions to have exerted pressure on the state government, as they clearly have in some states, to raise tuition in public institutions. In fact, if we ignore the two jurisdictions

---

[8] See Carnegie Commission (1974, Table 3), where the relationship is expressed in constant dollars.

(Massachusetts and the District of Columbia) in which enrollment in private institutions exceeds 50 percent of total enrollment, we find a rather consistent positive relationship between
the percentage of enrollment in private institutions and average
tuition and required fees in public two-year colleges (Figure
1).[9] This same relationship holds for public universities and for
public comprehensive universities and colleges.

We also found a fairly clear pattern of regional variations
in average state tuition and required fees (Figure 2 and Table 5).
Charges tend to be highest in the Middle Atlantic states and
relatively high also in the East North Central states. On the
other hand, they are especially low in the Pacific states and
comparatively low in the Mountain and West South Central
states. The other regions tend to occupy an intermediate position. But these regional variations are clearly related to percentages of enrollment in private higher education, as the bottom
row in Table 5 indicates. The largest proportions of enrollment
in private higher education are found generally in the north-
eastern section of the country, while the strongest traditions of
public higher education are found west of the Mississippi River
and especially in the Far West. The Northeast or New England
states, with their high proportion of enrollment in private
higher education, deviate somewhat from the general pattern of

[9]Massachusetts is something of a special case. Among its many private institutions of higher education are some of the most prestigious universities
and colleges in the nation. They draw their students from all over the
country and have high ratios of applicants to admissions. Thus their enrollment is not threatened by the presence of low-cost public institutions. For
this reason, there may have been less effective pressure on the state government to raise public tuition in Massachusetts than in certain other states in
which private institutions have considered themselves more uniformly
threatened by the competition of low-cost public institutions. In any
event, the Massachusetts Board of Higher Education conducted a major
study of tuition in 1970-71 and came to the conclusion that any increase
in student tuition should be opposed (Education Commission of the
States, 1971, p. 105).

The District of Columbia is obviously also a special case. Recently,
there have been strong moves to provide low-cost public higher education
there. Moreover, its major four-year institutions are its five private universities, which are not in direct competition to any appreciable extent with
its one public community college.

Figure 1. Average tuition and required fees in public colleges and
universities, by percent of total state enrollment in private institutions

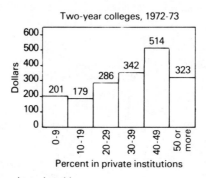

Two-year colleges, 1972-73

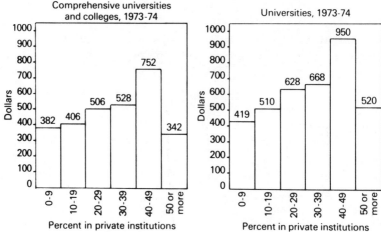

Comprehensive universities
and colleges, 1973-74

Universities, 1973-74

Percent in private institutions

Sources: Tables 4, 9, and 13.

variation in tuition charges, but the two largest states in the
region—Connecticut and Massachusetts—have maintained comparatively low charges in public two-year colleges and thus are
exceptions to the general tendency for charges to be high in
states with large proportions of enrollment in private institutions.

Not only does tuition, in general, tend to be relatively high
in public two-year colleges in states with strong private sectors,

Figure 2. Average tuition in public two-year colleges, by region, 1972-73

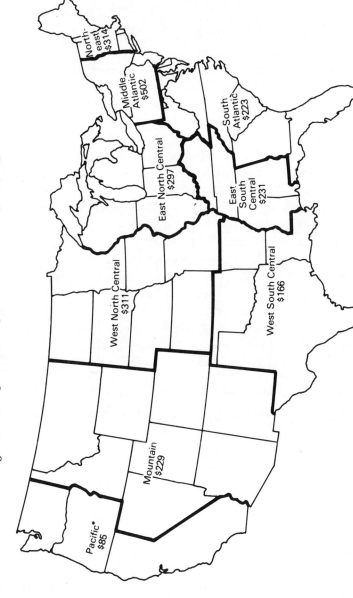

North-
east
$314

Middle
Atlantic
$502

East North Central
$297

South
Atlantic
$223

East
South
Central
$231

West North Central
$311

West South Central
$166

Mountain
$229

Pacific*
$85

*Includes Alaska and Hawaii.

Source: Table 5.

but these also tend to be the states that are spending comparatively sizable amounts on state scholarship programs. We shall
consider these programs in Section 5.

Tuition Changes in Recent Years

Although there has been an upward trend in tuition and required fees in public two-year colleges, along with other groups
of institutions in higher education, changes in recent years have
by no means followed a uniform pattern from state to state
(Table 6). Between 1968-69 and 1972-73, there were nine states
in which the average annual rate of increase exceeded 10 percent. In a very different category were four jurisdictions—Arizona, California, the District of Columbia, and Hawaii—that
were maintaining either no tuition or annual tuition charges of
less than $100. In the six states in which average tuition and
required fees declined during the four-year period, the usual
explanation was the establishment of new, relatively low-cost
institutions rather than actual reductions in charges in existing
institutions. The most significant example was Wisconsin, where
the number of two-year technical institutes with zero tuition
and low fees increased between 1968 and 1973. However, by
far the most states—30 in all—were those in which average tuition and required fees rose at rates varying from slightly more
than zero to less than 10 percent.

How Low Is "Low Tuition"?

Thus far, we have referred to a goal of "low or no tuition" without defining what we mean by "low."

Any answer to this question must be essentially arbitrary
and cannot be expected to be appropriate for the indefinite
future, regardless of changes in educational costs and in average
ability to pay. Nevertheless, in view of the widespread and
apparently growing support for the concept of open-door community colleges as the predominant type of open-access institution in the United States, we believe that there would be substantial agreement on defining "low" tuition in public two-year
colleges at a level somewhat below that which might be regarded
as "low" for lower-division students in four-year institutions.

For illustrative purposes, let us explore a possible standard for low or no tuition in public two-year colleges under which total annual tuition and required fees might range from zero to $150. We shall not attempt to specify how much of such a total charge might consist of tuition and how much of required fees. Where the institution is on a quarter system, as many are, this would involve a maximum charge of $50 a quarter for each of the three quarters of an academic year. On a semester system, it would amount to $75 a term.

State or Federal Implementation?

What are the probabilities that states might be induced to move toward a nationwide policy of low or no tuition in public two-year colleges, in the absence of some type of federal subsidy designed to induce tuition reductions? On the whole, they do not appear to be very high.

It is true that state fiscal positions improved substantially between the late 1960s and very early 1970s, when we became accustomed to thinking of the states as relatively unlikely sources of substantial new financing. Moreover, the Brookings Institution report on the 1974 federal budget predicted that during the following decade the increase in state and local revenues "should slightly outpace the increased expenditures necessitated by population growth, inflation, and a moderate improvement in service levels" (Fried et al., 1973, p. 270).[10] One of the sources of increased revenue would be the general revenue-sharing funds provided by the federal government

[10]The report cited five reasons for more favorable state and local fiscal positions: (1) slower population growth; (2) several new federal programs that would or could replace state expenditures with federal expenditures (federal supplemental income security payments for the aged, disabled, and blind and the student-aid provisions of the Educational Amendments of 1972); (3) the probability of a somewhat more moderate rate of increase in public employee compensation, as compared with the marked gains of the 1960s; (4) gradual changes in the revenue structure of states and localities toward taxes that are more responsive to economic growth; and (5) the general revenue-sharing program enacted in 1972, which would give state and local governments roughly $6 billion a year even if not expanded further.

under 1972 legislation. In 1973-74, $6 billion flowed to state
and local governments under general revenue-sharing—one-third
to state governments and two-thirds to local governments.

This more favorable outlook for the states is likely to be
temporarily reversed during the current economic recession, but
could well reappear if the recession is not too prolonged. Even
so, it seems unlikely that states in which tuition and fees in public two-year colleges have been rising—and this means, as we
have seen, the great majority of the states—will reverse this
trend in the face of costs which can be expected to continue to
rise. Resistance to any strong move toward reducing tuition and
fees in public two-year colleges would probably be most pronounced, our analysis suggests, in states with substantial propor
tions of total enrollment in private institutions.

Another complication in many of the states is the role of
local community college districts in decisions relating to tuition
and fees, as well as in the financing of community colleges.
State authorities desiring to move toward uniformly lower tuition would probably be faced with the necessity of increasing
the state's relative contribution to the public support of two-
year colleges in many of the states.

On the other hand, the growing popularity of low-cost
community colleges may result in political pressure in at least
some of the states to reverse rising trends in their student
charges. All things considered, however, it seems unlikely that
such pressure would be pervasive enough to bring about any-
thing resembling a nationwide movement toward lower tuition.

Alternative Federal Aid Formulas

If federal financial support would be needed to bring about a
nationwide move toward low or no tuition in public two-year
colleges, what sort of federal aid provisions would be most
appropriate?

First of all, we would suggest that any federal aid designed
to induce lower tuition should flow to the states rather than to
individual institutions of higher education. Decisions relating to
tuition in public higher education have rested with the states, or
have involved some combination of decision-making between

state and local authorities in the case of public two-year colleges or between states and boards of trustees in the case of public four-year institutions. We believe that intrusion of the federal government into this decision-making process through aid to institutions that would be conditional on lower tuition charges or on maintaining them at existing low levels would be undesirable. It could very well lead to greater federal government involvement in monitoring costs in higher education—a development that would widely be regarded as a threat to institutional autonomy.[11] In addition, decisions about tuition levels in public institutions are closely related to decisions about state aid to private institutions, whether in the form of student aid or institutional aid. Because of the wide variations in the relative enrollments of private institutions, and in the characteristics of private institutions, from state to state, there is a strong case for leaving these decisions with the states.

Colleges and universities are not concerned over federal monitoring of costs because they have an irresponsible attitude toward their expenditures. Financial stringency in recent years has forced both public and private institutions to economize wherever possible, and public institutions are being subjected to increasing state scrutiny of costs and programs. The fear is that federal involvement in monitoring of costs could threaten diversity and flexibility, leading perhaps to a deadly uniformity in programs. A college, for example, that had developed a special strength in a particular field might have great difficulty in maintaining that strength in the face of federal pressure toward adhering to certain cost-per-student standards. There are state pressures in this direction, but state pride in the quality of its public institutions has tended to act as something of a counterforce.

Second, because of the substantial variations in average tuition and fee charges from state to state, federal aid should not take the form of reimbursing states for all or any particular

[11]Reactions to even the mild suggestions for increased federal government involvement in collecting data on costs made by the National Commission on the Financing of Postsecondary Education indicated how widespread the concern over such a threat was.

share of the cost of reducing tuition in public two-year institutions. Such an approach would penalize the states in which tuition charges are now zero or very low and reward states in which charges are now high.

This leaves two other types of formulas under which federal aid might be granted for this purpose: (1) capitation payments to states based on full-time equivalent enrollment or (2) federal grants-in-aid to states based on formulas that might be related to such factors as the number of high school graduates, the number of persons aged 18 to 24 or, perhaps, aged 18 to 34, and an appropriate measure of state expenditure effort. Either capitation payments or federal grants-in-aid could be made conditional on reducing tuition and fees, or could be made conditional on a combination of objectives, such as reducing tuition and fees and maintaining open-door admissions policies in public two-year colleges. States already meeting the objectives would benefit by receiving federal funds that they could use either for reduction of state and/or local subsidies or for improving quality and programs.

Capitation payments to institutions of higher education—that is, so many dollars per FTE student, perhaps differentiated by level of education—became highly controversial during debates preceding the enactment of the Education Amendments of 1972. Supported by most of the associations representing colleges and universities, it was not the type of federal institutional aid preferred by the Carnegie Commission. The Commission favored major emphasis on grants to low-income students, accompanied by cost-of-education supplements *per student grant-holder* to institutions enrolling those students. The federal government, the Commission argued, had a special responsibility to promote equality of opportunity: "The highest single priority for federal funding in higher education in the 1970s is to help fulfill the two-century-old American dream of social justice" (Carnegie Commission, 1972, p. 2).

Capitation payments, also, would involve the federal government in supporting higher education in the same manner that has traditionally been used by the states and would lead inevitably to efforts by the states to induce the federal government to assume a steadily rising proportion of total support: "This would be the initial step toward a nationalized system as, first, the states would reduce their sense of basic responsibility, and, second, controls would inevitably follow the lump-sum across-the-board grants" (ibid.).

The principle of federal aid based on grants to low-income students accompanied by cost-of-education supplements was adopted as provided for under the Education Amendments of 1972, although thus far the cost-of-education supplements have not been funded.

For our present purposes, we may ask whether capitation payments to states for the specific purpose of inducing tuition reductions would involve the same dangers as across-the-board institutional payments. They might not involve comparable dangers for several reasons: (1) they would flow to states rather than to institutions and would be conditional on tuition reductions and possibly other policy changes and (2) they *could* be adopted only for a temporary period while such changes were being carried out, although on this basis, of course, states and local jurisdictions would ultimately have to bear the total cost of tuition reductions. On the other hand, there are several arguments in favor of grants-in-aid to the states based on factors other than existing FTE enrollment. These arguments will be considered at a later point.

For illustrative purposes, let us consider the cost and some of the implications of federal grants to states amounting to $100 per year per FTE student in public two-year colleges, conditional on reducing tuition and required fees to $150 a year within a specified period, say, three years. The total annual cost, using 1973-74 enrollment figures, would be about $179 million a year if all states participated.[12] The impact on states

---

[12] In 1973-74, there were 1,285 thousand full-time students and 1,509 thousand part-time students in public two-year colleges. Using the NCES formula under which each part-time student is counted as one-third of a full-time student, FTE enrollment was 1,788 thousand. (Actually, in the case of non-degree-credit students, the NCES formula counts a part-time as 28 percent of a full-time student, but data are not yet available in sufficient detail to make this adjustment, and it would make little difference in our result.)

would be as follows (usii.g 1972-73 data on tuition and required
fees from Table 1, in the absence of sufficient data for
1973-74):

· Eight states (including the District of Columbia), with average
  tuition and required fees of less than $150, would be able to
  use their allocations for purposes other than net reduction of
  tuition and fees (although a few adjustments would have to
  be made in institutions with charges exceeding $150).
· In 14 states, with tuition and required fees averaging from
  $150 to $250, the $100 payment would suffice to bring aver-
  age charges down to or below $150 as long as the federal
  grants continued, but again there would have to be some
  reductions exceeding $100 in individual institutions with
  charges above $250. On the other hand, many states with
  average charges in the lower part of the $150 to $250 range
  would receive substantial sums that could be used for purposes other than reduction of their charges.
· In the remaining states, with tuition and required fees of
  $250 or more, the federal allocations would not suffice to
  offset the full cost of reducing average tuition and required
  fees to $150, and state or local sources of funds would have
  to be developed to effectuate the full reduction. The higher
  the average charges in these states, the larger the amounts per
  FTE student that would have to be raised from state or local
  sources, and the more likely would be a decision on the part
  of the state not to participate in the tuition-reduction program. The problem of achieving the required reduction
  would, of course, be somewhat eased for these states by
  allowing the reduction to be effected over a period of several
  years, and the chances are that some of the states in this
  group would be induced to participate in the federal program,
  even though they would have to contribute significantly to
  the cost of tuition reductions. The experience with the State
  Student Incentive Grant program suggests the effectiveness of
  federal matching grants in inducing states to increase expenditures for higher education, but it must be kept in mind that
  the sums involved in most of the states thus far are far smaller

than the amounts that would be required to finance tuition reductions. Furthermore, a very substantial state movement toward student-aid programs was under way, as we shall see, before the federal provisions were enacted. But the fact that both scholarship expenditures and tuition levels tend to be highest in states with large private sectors suggests that there might be resistance in states with relatively high tuition levels to participation in a federal program aimed at tuition reduction, whereas those same states would welcome federal contributions to their scholarship programs.

In other words, we are led to the somewhat paradoxical result that states with the highest tuition charges would be least likely to participate in the program, and yet this is probably an inevitable result of the need for even-handed federal treatment of the states in a situation in which states and local districts have had widely differing tuition policies. To the extent that states did not participate, the federal cost would be reduced.

Capitation payments would take no account of differences in the fiscal capacity of states, as measured, for example, by per capita income. President Truman's Commission on Higher Education recommended federal grants to the states for both operating and capital costs of higher education to assist in achieving the objectives outlined in its report, including elimination of tuition and required fees in the first two years of public higher education. The grants for operating costs were to be allocated to the states "on an equalization basis, in accordance with an objective formula designed to take account of the relative needs of the States for higher education and their relative abilities to finance those needs" (The President's Commission, 1947, vol. 5, p. 5). Such formulas have, of course, been used in other federal grant-in-aid programs.

We shall defer a comparison of the implications of such a formula with those of capitation payments until Section 5.

3

Public Four-Year
Institutions

Many of the arguments supporting a policy of low or no tuition in public two-year colleges may also be used to support a policy of low or no tuition for lower-division students in public four-year institutions—for example, the uncertainty of many students about their probabilities of success in higher education during the first two years and the desirability of minimizing the extent to which students need to face the procedures involved in demonstrating need for student aid in those years.

Easing the path of adults wishing to participate in postsecondary education is another argument that applies about as strongly to the public four-year institutions as to the two-year colleges. Furthermore, there is concern over the tendency of existing tuition differentials and differential selection policies to encourage relative concentration of low-income and minority-group students in community colleges.

On the other hand, most private colleges and universities probably would view a move toward a national policy of low or no tuition in the first two years of *all* public higher education with greater alarm than a move confined to public two-year colleges. Most private institutions compete more directly with public four-year institutions than with public two-year colleges for their students, although this is less true of certain large private urban universities that have attributed some of their enrollment problems in recent years to the competition of low-cost public community colleges. Nevertheless, it is likely that a policy of low or no tuition in the first two years of all public higher education would be difficult to implement in the absence of substantially increased aid to private institutions, whether or not such aid was deliberately designed to facilitate a parallel policy of low or no tuition in the first two years of private higher education.

President Truman's Commission on Higher Education recommended the elimination of tuition and required fees in the first two years of all public higher education without any discussion of the problems this would pose for private higher education. The relative position of private higher education was far stronger in 1947 than it is today, and private colleges and universities accounted for about one-half of all enrollment in higher education at that time, as compared with less than one-fourth at present. Their tuition charges were also only a little more than twice those of public institutions immediately following World War II, as contrasted with charges that were more than three times those of public institutions in the 1930s and that average about five times those of public institutions today.[1] The relatively low ratio of private to public tuition charges in the immediate postwar years reflected the fact that, although both groups of institutions increased tuition relatively sharply during those years in response both to rising costs and to availability of direct tuition payments from the federal government for veterans, the rate of increase in public institutions was more pronounced than in private institutions.

Another highly significant difference between the situation in 1947 and at present is that states in which private higher education had historically been predominant—especially Massachusetts and New York—had barely begun to develop public systems of higher education, whereas they now have strong and growing public systems. To a considerable extent, this contrast between the two periods can also be found in other states. Thus, in 1947 private colleges and universities were competing

[1] See the table in Carnegie Commission (1974, p. 47).

less than today with public institutions for students *within the same state.*

In several of its reports, the Carnegie Commission recommended relatively low tuition in the first two years of public higher education.[2] In fact, both public and private four-year institutions were urged to restructure their tuition charges, so that there would be three levels of charges—the lowest for lower-division students, an intermediate level for upper-division students, and the highest level for graduate students. Thus, tuition charges would be more closely related to differences in educational costs per student and might eventually reach "a general level equal to about one-third of educational costs" (Carnegie Commission, 1973b, p. 109).

Howard Bowen, however, who is an advocate of low tuition in public higher education, while commending the moderate character of the Carnegie Commission recommendations on tuition policy, expressed some reservations about restructuring tuition charges in favor of lower-division students:

> This proposal raises some philosophical questions about the allocations of expenditures among the various levels of instruction and about the unity of the university. And it raises practical questions about potential effects on attrition with stepped-up tuition after two years or four years, and about competitive relationships between the private and public sector. If the plan applied to both private and public institutions as proposed, it could greatly widen the dollar gap between private and public tuitions for advanced students (Bowen, 1974, p. 14).

Before considering more fully a possible standard for low tuition in public four-year institutions, we need to examine variations in their current charges, as we have done for the two-year institutions. We shall distinguish between public universities and public comprehensive universities and colleges, as classified by the Carnegie Commission, because there is a tendency for the

[2] See Carnegie Commission (1971; and 1973b).

universities to have somewhat higher tuition charges than comprehensive universities and colleges, and there is probably a case for continuation of this differential. Comprehensive universities and colleges tend to be somewhat less selective than universities and to draw their students from families with relatively modest incomes and from relatively nearby localities to a greater extent than do universities.

In 1973-74, tuition and required fees at public universities averaged $576 (Table 7), and the great majority of these institutions had charges ranging from $400 to $700. However, there were 11 public universities with charges of less than $400 and 20 with tuition and required fees ranging upward from $700 to amounts exceeding $1,000. Three university systems had recently established lower tuition for lower-division than for upper-division students—the University of Michigan, the State University of New York, and the University of Wisconsin System. But these changes were made in connection with tuition increases, and did not result in particularly low tuition for lower-division students—at the University of Michigan charges at the two levels were $800 and $904, at SUNY they were $750 and $900, and at Wisconsin they were $573 and $628.[3]

Unlike the case of community colleges, there are no local boards of trustees involved in the governance of public universities and four-year colleges, except in the case of the City University of New York and a few other universities that were originally established as municipal institutions. Tuition charges are set by a state agency—whether it be the legislature, a state board, or the board of trustees of the institution or system—and almost invariably involve two sets of charges, one for state residents and a higher level of charges for students who cannot qualify as state residents.[4]

It is not surprising, then, that, on the whole, there is less

---

[3]These differing charges are not shown in the National Center for Educational Statistics *Directory,* but do appear in the 1973-74 report on student charges compiled by the National Association of State Universities and Land-Grant Colleges.

[4]CUNY, however, has no tuition and modest fees for city residents and a considerably higher set of charges for both state residents who do not reside in New York City and out-of-state students.

intrastate variation in tuition and required fees of public universities than of public two-year colleges. Interstate variations are pronounced, however, and reflect some of the same influences that we found to be important in the case of the two-year colleges. Differences in proportions of revenue received from local sources are irrelevant, because very few institutions receive any revenue from local sources. Somewhat surprisingly, moreover, there is no consistent tendency for tuition and required fees of public universities to rise with increases in state per capita personal income (see Tables 8 through 10). But there is a decided tendency, as we saw in Figure 1, for these charges to rise with increases in the proportion of total state enrollment in private institutions, although once again Massachusetts is an exception to the general pattern.[5] Average tuition and required fees in 1973-74 varied from $419 in states with less than 10 percent of their enrollment in private institutions to $950 in states with 40 to 49 percent of their enrollment in the private sector. And, again, the regional pattern of variation was very similar to that found in the case of the two-year colleges, although the Pacific states were relatively higher in the spectrum in the case of public universities than in the case of two-year colleges.

Tuition and required fees tend to be somewhat lower in public comprehensive universities and colleges (state colleges) than in public universities, but the differences, for the most part, are not very pronounced (Table 11).[6] In 1973-74, average charges in the comprehensive institutions were $459, and the range of state averages was from $132 in the District of Columbia to $810 in Vermont. Nearly 65 percent of these institutions were in a middle group with charges ranging from $300 to $599, while 17 percent had charges below $300 and 18 percent had tuition and required fees ranging upward from $600 to more than $800.

[5] The District of Columbia has no public university and thus is not included in Table 9.

[6] For purposes of all relevant tables in this report, institutions are classified according to the Carnegie Commission classification. For definitions of the various categories and the classified list of institutions, see Carnegie Commission (1973a). The unit is in most cases, a campus, rather than a multicampus system.

Factors influencing interstate variations are very similar to those found in the case of public universities and require no additional comment (see Tables 12 through 14).

A Standard for Low Tuition

Consistent with a point of view expressed at various points in this report, we do not believe that the federal government should use a percentage of lower-division educational costs as a standard for determining what is meant by low tuition in the first two years of public four-year institutions. Such a standard would involve the federal government in monitoring costs—a development which we view as undesirable. It is true that the Carnegie Commission suggested charges amounting to about one-third of educational costs at each level at public four-year institutions, but this recommendation was made as a guide to states, and not in the context of a federal program directly designed to induce tuition reductions.

Adoption of as low a standard as the ceiling of $150 that was discussed earlier for public two-year institutions would require a considerably larger increase in public subsidies per FTE student in the four-year institutions because of their higher existing tuition charges.

Again, for illustrative purposes, and not necessarily as a serious policy proposal, let us consider possible maxima of $250 for the comprehensive universities and colleges and $350 for public universities. These ceilings would be considerably below current average charges for the two groups of institutions.

In the case of the comprehensive universities and colleges, a federal contribution of $200 per FTE student would be roughly comparable, in relation to the current average tuition and required fees of $459 and the suggested ceiling of $250, to the $100 per FTE student we discussed for the public two-year colleges, with their average tuition and fees of $252 and the suggested ceiling of $150. With approximately 820,000 FTE lower-division students enrolled in these institutions in 1973-74, the cost of such a federal subvention would be about $164 million, if all states participated. The implications for states in relation to existing tuition and fee levels would be about as follows:

- Only in California, the District of Columbia, and Hawaii were 1973-74 average charges below $250. These jurisdictions could use the federal subvention of $200 per FTE student to replace existing state subsidies, reduce charges somewhat below current levels voluntarily, and/or improve quality of programs. The same comments apply to the CUNY four-year institutions, but the federal subvention in this case would probably be shared in some manner by the state and New York City, both of which participate in the financing of CUNY.
- There would be 20 states with tuition and required fees ranging from $250 to $450, in which a federal subvention amounting to $200 per FTE student would fully meet the cost—at 1973-74 levels—of reducing average tuition and fees to $250. A good many of these states with average tuition and fees below $450 would be able to use a substantial part of the federal funds for other purposes.
- This would leave 28 states in which $200 per FTE student would not suffice to meet the cost of reducing average tuition and fees to $250. (In New York this would be true only for SUNY colleges.) As in the case of public two-year colleges, the higher existing tuition and fee levels are, the more likely would be a decision on the part of a state not to participate in the federal program. Some of the states in this group might decide to raise at least part of the funds required to reduce lower-division tuition by raising tuition for upper-division and graduate students.

In addition, of course, states would have to meet future increases in costs in order to maintain their lower-division tuition and fee charges below the suggested ceiling, unless the federal capitation payments were regularly adjusted upward to reflect increases in costs.

Turning to the public universities, a capitation grant of $225 would be comparable in relation to tuition levels to those we have discussed for the other two groups of institutions. Again, the impact on the states would vary greatly in accordance with their differing tuition levels. These differences would be very similar to those relating to comprehensive universities and colleges and will not be set forth in detail.

A complication in the case of the public universities is the fact that they tend to have relatively more students from other states and foreign countries than either the comprehensive universities and colleges or the two-year colleges. In order not to widen the already large difference between tuition for state residents and out-of-state students, capitation payments could be made for out-of-state students and nonresident tuition decreased by the same dollar amount as resident tuition, or out-of-state students could be given special tuition grants reflecting the amount of the reduction. There would be complications in states in which tuition for state residents would not need to be reduced or would need to be reduced by considerably less than the amount of the capitation payment. A formula might be worked out which would call for reductions in nonresident and resident tuition differentials where these are exceptionally high. However, as a result of recent court decisions there has been a tendency to give out-of-state students the right to be classified as state residents after one year of study in a given state, and thus the number of students paying nonresident tuition is declining relatively.[7]

The number of lower-division FTE students in public universities in 1973-74 was about 903,000, and thus the cost of a $225 capitation payment would be about $203 million annually, if all states participated.

In the previous section, we called attention to the upward trend in tuition charges in public two-year colleges in the majority of states. The fact that there has also been a sharp upward trend in tuition charges of public four-year colleges and universities in recent years is familiar and scarcely needs emphasis.[8] The prospect for a reversal of these trends, as suggested earlier, is not at all promising.

[7] See Carnegie Commission (1974, pp. 21-22).

[8] In the case of the four-year institutions, as at the two-year colleges, however, there have been substantial variations among the states in rates of increase. See Carnegie Commission (1974, Tables 6 and 7).

In this connection, however, the recent recommendation of the Board of Regents of the University of Wisconsin System for a 50 percent reduction in undergraduate tuition at the system's four-year campuses—from 25 percent to 12.5 percent of educational costs per student—is of considerable interest, although it is not at all clear that the recommendation will be accepted by the legislature or by Governor Patrick J. Lucey, who spoke against the proposal during his campaign for reelection ("Cutting Tuition in Half," 1974). The regents believe tuition reductions might reverse the recent trend toward declining enrollment on a number of the system's four-year campuses—especially campuses of the former state colleges—in contrast with increasing enrollments at many of the two-year technical institutes, which, as we saw in Section 2, have no tuition and very modest fees (University of Wisconsin System, 1974). Whether these contrasting trends can be attributed entirely to tuition differentials, however, is somewhat problematical.[9] Even so, the Wisconsin proposal may conceivably be a forerunner of similar developments in other public systems that are facing declining or sluggish enrollment.

In Section 5, we shall consider alternative formulas for possible allocations of federal grants to the states, as well as the impact of increased enrollment that might be induced by lower tuition, but we need first to turn our attention to the question of private institutions.

---

[9]Other factors that have probably also played a role, as they have nationally, are (1) the change in the draft situation, which has been a factor explaining the sharp decline in college enrollment rates of youthful males in recent years; (2) the unfavorable job market for teachers, which has discouraged enrollment at public four-year colleges that have been heavily oriented toward teacher-training; and (3) the relatively favorable job market in the allied health professions and in other occupational fields for which training is provided in two-year colleges and technical institutes. Even the much-publicized sharp increases in enrollment at the Fond du Lac and Rice Lake two-year university centers, following drastic reductions in their tuition charges, may represent, at least to some extent, diversions of enrollment of students who would otherwise have enrolled at one of the four-year campuses rather than net additions to enrollment in the system.

4

Private
Institutions

The problem of implementing a national policy of low or no tuition for lower-division students in private institutions is much more complex than is the case in public institutions. Average tuition and required fees in private colleges and universities were estimated at $2,095 in 1973-74 by the U.S. National Center for Educational Statistics (NCES) (1974c, p. 110). The going rate in some of the most selective private institutions is $3,000 or more (Suchar, Van Dusen, and Jacobson, 1974). Thus capitation grants of the amounts we have been discussing would not go very far toward inducing policies of low or no tuition for lower-division students in private institutions, even if they were made applicable to private institutions.[1]

Assuming uniform capitation payments were provided to states for lower-division students in both public and private

---

[1] Any suggestion that capitation payments might be made higher for private than for public institutions might raise questions as to constitutionality. There are, however, legal ways in which private institutions have been indirectly favored, such as the larger amounts per student provided for smaller institutions under the cost-of-education supplement provisions of the Education Amendments of 1972, which tend to favor private institutions because of their smaller average size.

It is true, also, that the federal Basic Educational Opportunity Grants program, in which aid is related to cost of attendance, can provide higher amounts to students attending private institutions, but the aid flows through students, rather than directly to institutions.

institutions, there might also be legal questions about whether the states could make capitation payments to private institutions conditional on lowering tuition. However, it would be possible for the federal government to make capitation payments to states for lower-division students in private institutions as well as in public institutions and leave it to the states to determine whether these funds would flow to the private institutions in the form of student aid or institutional subsidies. There would be some states that would not need to use all of the federal subventions for tuition reductions in the public sector—indeed, some that would not need to use any of the federal funds for that purpose, at least for some types of public institutions—and presumably these states could allocate to the private sector more than the total amount of capitation grants based on FTE enrollment in private institutions. However, these possibilities would probably be limited because of the correlation we have found between tuition levels in the public sector and the relative importance of private enrollment in the state.

In the typical case, private colleges and universities would be assisted in adjusting to a reduction of tuition in public institutions through capitation payments or equivalent allocations to students, but the tuition *gap* between private and public institutions would not be reduced. Although it is difficult to predict how private institutions would react to the type of program under discussion, in many cases they would probably prefer liberalization of state student-aid programs, along with direct state aid to private institutions, as compared with state participation in a federal grants program aimed at reduction of tuition. This would be particularly true in states in which tuition in public higher education is relatively high, and in which the tuition reductions required by the federal program would therefore be large.

In this connection, one of the notable tendencies of recent years has been a pronounced increase in the number of state student-aid programs and in the amounts expended on them. The most recent survey by the National Association of State Scholarship Programs indicates that in the fall of 1974 there were 36 states with comprehensive undergraduate state scholarship or grant programs in operation (Winkler, 1974). A decade earlier, only about 10 states had such programs, and these were frequently very limited. Not only has the number of states with such programs been increasing rapidly, but some of the states that started with very limited programs have added more comprehensive programs in recent years. Total expenditures on these programs increased from an estimated $44 million in 1963-64 to about $456 million in 1974-75 (Carnegie Commission, 1973b, p. 162; and Winkler, 1974).[2]

Some of these programs, though a minority of the total, are limited to the provision of tuition grants for students attending private institutions only. According to Millard (1974), a major portion of the aid in 1973-74 went to students in private institutions.

Amounts made available under these programs tend to vary with the percentage of state enrollment in private institutions. In terms of appropriations per enrolled student, the amounts available were less than $10 in some of the states, but amounted to more than $100 in Illinois, New Jersey, New York, and Pennsylvania (Table 15). Average amounts available per enrolled student (including students in states with no programs or with zero appropriations) rose almost steadily from $3.91 in states with less than 10 percent of enrollment in private institutions to $122.38 in states with 40 to 49 percent of enrollment in private institutions (Table 16). Once again, Massachusetts and the District of Columbia (the two jurisdictions with more than 50 percent of enrollment in private institutions) were exceptions to the general tendency.[3]

In fiscal year 1974-75, funds were available for the first time, in the amount of $19 million, for the State Student Incentive Grant program that was adopted under the federal Educa-

---

[2] The latter figure represents total appropriations, rather than actual expenditures.

[3] Appropriations per enrolled student have been used to measure the comparative amounts available under these programs, rather than average amount of aid received by students receiving awards, because the eligibility conditions vary greatly from state to state. An alternative measure might be appropriations per member of the 18- to 21-year-old population.

tion Amendments of 1972. Under this new program, the federal government provides grants to the states to meet 50 percent of amounts of student aid provided under state programs that meet criteria set forth in the act. These criteria are (1) administration by a single state agency, (2) a maximum grant of $1,500 for attendance on a full-time basis as an undergraduate in an institution of higher education, (3) selection of recipients of grants on the basis of substantial financial need, and (4) maintenance of previous state appropriations for student-aid programs. Availability of federal matching funds has apparently stimulated a number of additional states to adopt student-aid programs. By September 1974, there were 41 states with programs that qualified for federal allotments, and all of the remaining 9 states were considering adoption of such programs. Five of the 41 states with programs had not yet appropriated funds. States with existing programs were restructuring them to meet the federal criteria.

Programs of direct institutional aid to private colleges and universities are much less numerous than student-aid programs, but have been adopted in a number of states in relatively recent years. By 1974 there were 14 states with direct institutional aid programs, not including the specialized programs for support of private medical, dental, and/or nursing schools which exist in a number of states (Education Commission of the States, 1974). Among those 14 states, however, only 8—Connecticut, Illinois, Maryland, Michigan, Minnesota, New Jersey, New York, and Oregon—had general programs of institutional aid to all private institutions. Pennsylvania had long provided substantial institutional aid to selected institutions. These states all have sizable private sectors of higher education.

The trend toward increased state aid to private institutions is significant in relation to the problem of implementing a national policy of low or no tuition in the first two years of higher education, because this trend has been associated with tuition increases in public higher education.

The cost of providing capitation payments to the states for FTE lower-division students enrolled in private institutions, equivalent at each major type of institution to those provided under our illustrative proposals for public institutions, is estimated at about $144 million on the basis of 1973-74 enrollment.

It should be emphasized that the amounts of tuition reduction and of capitation grants that we have discussed are for *illustrative purposes only*. They are not intended as serious policy proposals. The total cost of the capitation grants we have discussed on the basis of 1973-74 enrollment would be about $700 million if all states participated in the program, which is not likely. There *could* be offsetting savings in existing student-aid programs—to be discussed later.

The number of states that would probably decide not to participate could be quite large, as our analysis suggests. Doubling the amounts of the capitation grants, at a cost of $1.4 billion, would probably induce the majority of states to participate, but it would also involve providing rather large sums to states with low tuition levels—sums that they would not need to meet the proposed tuition standards. This dilemma might not be quite so clear under alternative formulas for federal grants to states, to which we now turn.

5

Alternative Formulas for Federal Grants to States

If the federal government were to adopt a broad program of grants-in-aid to the states, there would be much to be said for an allocation formula that would include features that would be designed more specifically to induce states to increase their expenditures on higher education, especially in those states in which such expenditures have lagged in the past. A traditional way of inducing increased state expenditure, of course, is through a program of federal matching grants, as in the State Student Incentive Grant program. However, matching grants are not appropriate as a means of inducing tuition reductions, because the amounts required for this purpose per FTE student would vary so greatly from state to state, that we would again face the dilemma noted at the start.

An Illustrative Formula

Historically, the states that have lagged in expenditures on higher education have been the states with relatively large proportions of enrollment in private higher education. This continued to be true in 1972-73—the latest year for which data on combined state and local expenditures for higher education are available. We have explored two measures of comparative state expenditure effort: (1) state and local expenditures as a percentage of total state personal income and (2) state and local expenditures per member of the population aged 18 to 21 as a percentage of per capita personal income. The relative ranking of most states does not vary greatly on the basis of these two measures, and we have used the first in an analysis of variations in state effort.[1] Strikingly, state expenditures on the basis of this measure varied from an average of 1.22 percent of personal income in states with 0 to 9 percent of their total state enrollment in private higher education to 0.60 percent in Massachusetts, the one state with more than 50 percent of its enrollment in private institutions (Table 17).[2] New York State was something of an exception to the general pattern, with 40 percent of its enrollment in private institutions in 1972 and expenditures amounting to 1.24 percent of personal income.

Some advocates of low tuition in public higher education also believe that the survival of private institutions—especially of the weaker private colleges and universities—is in jeopardy and that decisive moves should be made to strengthen the financial position of the private sector. However, they tend to oppose any move to improve the relative position of private institutions by reducing the tuition gap, arguing that private colleges and universities should, instead, receive increased public subsidies. For example, Roger W. Heyns, president of the American Council on Education, in a statement explaining the ACE position on tuition policy, commented:

> Tuition increases in public institutions have been proposed as a means of assisting private institutions. . . .
> ACE does not believe that accelerating the rate of increase in tuition will have the predicted effect. . . .

[1]Measures of state effort will be analyzed more extensively in a forthcoming report of the Carnegie Council on state policies toward higher education. It should be noted that expenditure data for 1972-73 have not as yet been published by the U.S. National Center for Educational Statistics, but we have been able to obtain the data from HEGIS tapes.

[2]We do not have 1972-73 expenditure data for the District of Columbia, in which private enrollment also amounts to more than 50 percent.

To help private education ACE endorses a policy
of basic public support for part of the costs of edu-
cating students in private institutions (American
Council on Education, 1974).

The Carnegie Commission advocated a very moderate increase in tuition in public higher education, except for the community colleges, but felt that the major thrust of the move to
preserve the private sector should come through increased state
aid to private institutions, particularly in the form of grants to
low-income students.[3]
To the extent that states with large private sectors continue to spend relatively large amounts on state scholarship programs—*and* increase those amounts to qualify for federal matching grants—they will receive relatively large shares of federal
funds under that program. However, we are here exploring the
possibility of an additional and broader program of federal
grants-in-aid to the states, which might be specifically designed
to accomplish a number of objectives:

1. Induce the states to pursue policies of low or no tuition for
   lower-division students in public higher education.
2. Induce the states that have lagged in financial support of
   postsecondary education to increase their relative effort. Because these tend to be states with relatively large proportions
   of total enrollment in private institutions, this could be a
   very significant way of inducing increased state support of
   private higher education.
3. Induce the states to make certain that a specified proportion
   of all student places conform to "open-access" criteria.

To accomplish all three of these objectives, federal grants-
in-aid could be made conditional on (1) lowering tuition in the
first two years of public higher education, along lines discussed
above, and perhaps providing capitation grants to private

---

[3] For a recent set of recommendations for increased public subsidies to
private institutions, see Association of American Colleges (1974).

colleges equivalent in dollar amount to tuition reductions in comparable public institutions; (2) pursuing policies designed to ensure that a certain proportion, say, one-third, of all student places conformed to open-access criteria; and (3) *for states that ranked below the average for the nation on the basis of an objective measure of state expenditure effort,* adopting a financing plan that would induce those states to increase the proportion of personal income spent on postsecondary education.

One possible formula might allocate one-half of federal funds in proportion to the number of persons aged 18 to 34 in each state and one-half in proportion to total FTE enrollment in higher education in each state. An adjustment might also be considered to provide a somewhat larger share of federal funds to states with low per capita incomes.

In order to be effective in accomplishing the three objectives mentioned above, the total federal annual appropriation for this program would probably need to be larger than the $700 million discussed for illustrative purposes in connection with a capitation grants program. An initial annual appropriation on the order of $2 billion, for example, would yield an average of $303 per FTE undergraduate on the basis of 1973 enrollment. The actual average received in any given state would, of course, vary from this amount in accordance with the formula suggested above, but, in most cases, the amounts made available would finance the suggested decreases in tuition in lower-division enrollment in public higher education and yield significant amounts for aid to private higher education in some form.

However, we have seen that states with relatively high tuition levels in public higher education also tend to be the states that fall below the national average on measures of expenditure effort, and that these tend to be states with comparatively high proportions of enrollment in private higher education. Thus, some of these states would probably not participate in the federal program because of the problems they would face in financing both the required tuition reductions and the required increases in state expenditure effort. Amounts that would be received by the various states under our illustrative formula are indicated in Table 18.

There are other difficulties involved in this approach to inducing increased state expenditures in states that are lagging. Thus far, only a small minority of state scholarship programs provide any aid for students attending college in other states. There may also be reluctance in some states to provide institutional aid on a capitation basis for out-of-state students enrolled in private institutions in the state. The whole question of the impact of such a program on interstate mobility of students requires careful consideration. One of the important advantages of the federal Basic Educational Opportunity Grants program is that it does not discourage interstate mobility except insofar as existing funding limitations and the 50 percent restriction on coverage of student costs hold down the amount qualified students receive. It should also be kept in mind that funding of the existing cost-of-education supplements would provide substantial aid to private institutions.

An approach to a federal grants-in-aid program that is very different from any of those discussed as yet might be one specifically designed to induce increases in enrollment rates. Grants could be made conditional on progress in raising enrollment rates and would *not* be conditional on tuition reductions, although conceivably tuition reductions might be one method that would be adopted by at least some states to bring about increased enrollment rates. Implementation of such a program would *require* an updated student interstate migration survey, because the objective would presumably be to increase enrollment rates of comparatively low-income state residents who would be unlikely to be in a position to attend college in another state. Thus, it would be important to have access to data on enrollment rates of state residents within each state.

Several points would have to be kept in mind in the design of such a policy. Analysis of 1970 census data indicates that enrollment rates tend to vary with state per capita income. Thus a formula aimed at increasing enrollment rates should probably include a factor that would favor relatively low per capita income states. Second, there is a high positive relationship between college enrollment rates and high school graduation rates among the states.[4] Expansion of federal expenditures on programs aimed directly at improving secondary education should be viewed as having high priority both in increasing high school graduation rates and in indirectly increasing college enrollment rates.[5]

Induced Enrollment and Savings in Student Aid

Before completing this analysis of various alternative approaches to federal aid to states, we need to take into account the probable savings in federal student aid that would be associated with any program designed to induce tuition reductions and the likelihood that any one of the alternative approaches that we have been discussing would induce increases in enrollment over those likely to occur without such a program.

Implementation of tuition reductions in public higher education would provide potential savings under existing federal and state student-aid programs by reducing the amounts of aid needed by lower-division students attending public institutions. However, we believe that both the BEOG program and the State Student Incentive Grants program should be far more adequately funded before such savings are considered as a basis for reducing appropriations under these programs. We have recently estimated that adequate funding of the BEOG program would call for an annual appropriation of $2 to $2.6 billion, depending on how many "extra" students are induced to enroll as a result of the availability of aid (Gordon, 1974).[6] Adequate funding of

---

[4]This relationship will be discussed more fully in our forthcoming report on state policies toward higher education.

[5]A program of federal grants to states suggested by Kirschling and Postweiler (1974) would, among other features, aim at increasing enrollment rates by rewarding states that already have relatively high enrollment rates with higher amounts per student than states with lower enrollment rates would receive. Whether such an approach would be as effective in inducing increases in enrollment rates as a policy under which federal grants would be, at least to some extent, conditional on increases in enrollment rates is somewhat questionable. This 1974 proposal involves some revisions of the earlier Kirschling-Postweiler (1971) proposal.

[6]This estimate agrees closely with estimates prepared by the Brookings Institution (Fried et al., 1973, p. 157).

the State Student Incentive Grants program would require at least the $50 million authorized in the 1972 legislation plus the amounts required under an open-ended authorization to finance the federal portion of continuing grants to students who received awards in previous years.

Assuming that these federal student-aid programs are eventually funded to this extent, we can attempt an estimate of the savings in student aid that could be expected partially to offset the cost of a federal program of grants to states designed to induce tuition reductions. We have considered programs that might vary in cost from about $700 million to perhaps $2 billion. In practice, the cost of a program designed simply to induce tuition reductions and based on a capitation formula would probably be reduced somewhat below $700 million, because some states would decide not to participate. Similarly, grants based on more complex formulas and designed to achieve a combination of purposes might involve somewhat reduced federal expenditures because of the nonparticipation of some of the states. Even in the simpler case of our $700 million program, estimates of actual costs and offsetting savings must include assumptions about which states would not participate. This is not easy to predict. Some informed persons have suggested that most states would be induced to participate in the program, even if they had to raise substantial amounts of funds to achieve the suggested tuition reductions. Others have been more skeptical. Probably the most important finding in our analysis of interstate tuition variations was that relatively high tuition levels in public institutions tended to be found in states with a relatively large proportion of total enrollment in private institutions. This means that the very states that would have to raise the largest sums per FTE student to achieve the suggested tuition reductions would also be states in which supporters of private institutions would oppose participation in the federal program.

Our staff has developed estimates that assume that six states—Indiana, Iowa, New Hampshire, Ohio, Pennsylvania, and Vermont—would decide not to participate in the program because of the large sums they would have to raise to achieve the suggested tuition reductions and because of possible opposition from their private sectors. On this basis, the cost of our illustrative program of federal grants would be reduced from about $700 to $650 million, and the estimated savings in federal student-aid expenditures would be about $260 million.[7]

However, the future cost of such a program would clearly be affected by any increase in enrollment attributable to the contemplated tuition reductions. Because tuition reductions would vary substantially from state to state, and existing estimates of the probable impact of tuition changes on enrollment are, in our opinion, not sufficiently refined to be capable of predicting student responses in individual states, given the widely varying "mixes" of various types of institutions in the states, we have not attempted to estimate the "extra" enrollment that might be induced by tuition reductions per se. The Council staff has developed several projections of enrollment that might occur under alternative assumptions, all involving conditions encouraging universal access to postsecondary education and involving adequate funding of existing student-aid provisions, among other changes. They imply increases in enrollment of varying amounts over our baseline projections, but are not directly applicable to the present discussion.

The most significant savings that can be anticipated in student-aid programs in the coming years will be reductions in expenditures for veterans' educational benefits as the flow of Vietnam veterans into higher education declines. These future savings should facilitate increasing federal aid to higher education under other programs.[8] Tuition reductions discussed in this

---

[7] A complication that is not taken into account in our estimate of student-aid savings is that students receiving veterans benefits or social security benefits would, in most instances, be eligible for only limited, if any, aid under the BEOG program or state scholarship programs. On the other hand, we have used 1971 enrollment data (the latest year for which detailed data are available) in estimating the savings estimate, whereas savings on the basis of 1973 enrollment data would be somewhat larger, so the errors are partially offsetting.

[8] From a practical political point of view, the fact that veterans benefits are considered by different congressional committees from those considering other federal aid programs is an obstacle to achievement of this result.

section would not, however, provide a basis for savings under the veterans' program itself, because Congress has not authorized the separate tuition benefits that have recently been under consideration, and there would be strong opposition to any reduction in the monthly amounts veterans currently receive.

Concluding Remarks

Because of the widespread interest in proposals for low or no tuition in the first two years of public postsecondary education, we have attempted a fairly extensive analysis of how such proposals might be implemented on a national basis, in the light of existing patterns of variations in tuition among the states and existing differences in state expenditure effort.

The analysis indicates that the prospects for state action to lower tuition in the first two years of public higher education *without federal assistance* are not promising, because of the pressure in many states, and especially in those with substantial proportions of enrollment in private higher education, toward measures that will encourage the survival of private higher education. These measures are taking the form both of tuition increases in public higher education and widespread adoption of state programs of aid to private higher education, chiefly, thus far, in the form of scholarship aid.

We have explored the possibility of federal assistance to stimulate state action toward lower tuition, either through a capitation grants program or through some alternative allocation formula. Progress toward lower tuition in the first two years of public higher education could be made through such an approach, but, unless the amounts allocated to the states were very large (that is, larger than those we have used for illustrative purposes), this approach would be least effective in the states with the highest existing tuition levels. This is an inevitable result of existing patterns of tuition variations in public higher education among the states.

Thus, federal government assistance designed to induce tuition reductions in the first two years of higher education in the states would be influential, but we know of no magic formula that would achieve a uniform national policy and at the same time maintain equitable treatment of the states and preserve their historical role in decisions about tuition and related financing matters. We have also explored the implications of low or no tuition in the first two years of public higher education on private institutions and have suggested that any move toward low or no tuition for lower-division students in public institutions should be accompanied by increased aid to private institutions in some form. As part of an inquiry into alternative paths to assistance of both public and private institutions, we have also explored a federal program of grants-in-aid to the states that would be designed both to encourage reduced tuition in the first two years of public higher education and to stimulate increased expenditures in states in which expenditures have lagged in the past—chiefly states with substantial proportions of enrollment in private higher education. Such a program might also be designed to encourage the provision of more open-access student places. Again, however, there are obstacles to clear-cut accomplishment of this combination of objectives, stemming from the fact that states that would require large tuition reductions also tend to be states that have been below average on measures of state effort.[9] There might also be undesirable side effects on interstate mobility of students. The analysis suggests the desirability of further exploration of federal grants-in-aid to the states, but tends to underscore some of the advantages of funding of the existing cost-of-education supplement provisions as a means of aiding both public and private institutions.

We have not explored the possibility of federal matching grants, but matching grants designed to induce the states to pursue certain policies would raise the same problems of equita-

---

[9] A very different approach to a federal policy aimed in part at maintaining low tuition in public colleges and universities has been proposed by Tirrell and McGuinness (1974) in a statement presented to the Special Subcommittee on Education, U.S. House of Representatives. Although their proposals include a number of features worthy of serious consideration, we have reservations about their proposed modifications in existing cost-of-education supplement provisions that would allocate tuition subsidies to institutions with tuition below $1,400 and that would limit future tuition increases in institutions benefiting from the supplements. As indicated earlier, we believe that decisions about tuition should be left to the states.

ble treatment that we have encountered from the start of this analysis. Matching grants have usually been used to induce the states to adopt new programs, in which equitable treatment is less difficult than in general support to higher education, in which the states have historically played the major role but have had different "mixes" of public and private higher education that have been associated with widely varying tuition policies and relative expenditures.

Finally, as the introductory statement to this report points out, we recognize the need for continued discussion and debate over possible improvements in existing federal legislation and have recently included some recommendations for modifications in our report, *The Federal Role in Postsecondary Education*. The most important of these recommendations are as follows:

1. Full funding of the Basic Educational Opportunity Grants program and of the Cost-of-Education Supplements program should be achieved by 1980.
2. The BEOG program should gradually be restructured so that the maximum grant equals 100 percent of a student's non-instructional costs, and student aid designed to help students meet instructional costs should be shifted to other programs.
3. Appropriations for the State Student Incentive Grants programs should be increased so that, by 1980, federal-state funds are adequate to provide full tuition grants to students from families in the lowest income quartile and one-half of tuition, on the average, to students from the next-to-lowest family income quartile.
4. A new program of federal matching funds for a Tuition Equalization Grants program should be adopted. The grants should be provided for all students attending private colleges and universities, and should, on the average, equal one-half of the educational subsidy at public four-year institutions.
5. Existing student loan programs should gradually be phased out and replaced by a National Student Bank.

Appendix

Earlier Relevant Recommendations of the Carnegie Commission on Higher Education

---

1. In *The Open-Door Colleges,* the Commission stated its belief that tuition charges in community colleges should be held to low levels and that, as federal aid is expended and the states strengthen their financial support of community colleges, a statewide no-tuition policy should be followed in as many states as possible. It was specifically recommended that *"states revise their legislation, wherever necessary, to provide for uniform low tuition or no tuition charges at public two-year colleges"* (1970, p. 46).

2. In *The Capitol and the Campus,* the Commission broadened this recommendation to call for no tuition or very low tuition in the first two years of *all public institutions,* including community colleges, state colleges, and universities. It also warned that, when public institutions found it necessary to raise tuition and other required fees, increases should be at no higher rate than increases in per capita personal disposable income. The Commission also recommended that states should not consider raising tuition levels at public institutions until after establishment of a tuition grants program (1971, pp. 85-86).

3. In *Higher Education: Who Pays? Who Benefits? Who Should Pay?* it was again recommended that public institutions—and especially community colleges—should maintain a relatively low-tuition policy for the first two years of higher education. It was also recommended that public colleges and universities should carefully study their educational costs per student and consider restructuring their tuition charges at upper-division and graduate levels to more nearly reflect the real differences in the cost of education per student, eventually reaching a general level equal to about one-third of educational costs.

This same recommendation for restructuring tuition charges in favor of lower-division students, and for progressively higher charges at upper-division and graduate levels, was also made for private institutions. Private colleges and universities, in addition, were urged not to increase their tuition charges more rapidly than per capita disposable income and, if possible, to hold increases below such a rate (1973b, pp. 108-110).

Statistical Tables

Table 1. Frequency distribution of tuition and required fees, public two-year colleges, by state, 1972-73

Tuition and required fees (in dollars)	United States	Alabama	Alaska	Arizona	Arkansas	California	Colorado	Connecticut	Delaware	District of Columbia	Florida
0	157			6		89	2				
1-99	42			5	2	6					
100-199	146			1		1	1			1	
200-299	232	18	8		3		10	13			19
300-399	196						2	3	3		5
400-499	96						1				
500-599	24										
600-699	22										
700-799	15										
800-899	18										
900-999											
1,000-1,099	1										
Number of institutions	948	18	8	12	5	96	16	16	3	1	28
Average tuition and required fees	252	203	200	48	187	2	232	229	390	90	244
Control*	S	S	S	S&L	M	S&L	M	S	S	F	S&L

Tuition and required fees (in dollars)	Georgia	Hawaii	Idaho	Illinois	Indiana	Iowa	Kansas	Kentucky	Louisiana	Maine	Maryland
0				10			1		1		
1-99		7		3					1		
100-199				5			1		3		
200-299	11		1	8				2	1		4
300-399	2		1	14	13	3	15	12		3	11
400-499				6		19	4			2	2
500-599				2							
600-699											
700-799					1						
800-899											
900-999											
1,000-1,099											
Number of institutions	13	7	2	48	14	22	21	14	6	5	17
Average tuition and required fees	281	50	298	232	365	410	220	367	121	340	305
Control*	S&L	S	S&L	S&L	S	S&L	S&L	S	M	S	S&L

(continued on next page)

Table 1 (*continued*)

Tuition and required fees (in dollars)	Massachusetts	Michigan	Minnesota	Mississippi	Missouri	Montana	Nebraska	Nevada	New Hampshire	New Jersey	New Mexico
0				1	1						1
1-99											
100-199				12	4	2	1			1	1
200-299	1	2		4	6	1	9		5		1
300-399	13	26	18	1			3	3	2	8	3
400-499		4	2		3					5	4
500-599										1	
600-699	2										
700-799											
800-899											
900-999											
1,000-1,099											
Number of institutions	16	32	20	18	14	3	13	3	7	15	10
Average tuition and required fees	337	337	373	181	241	185	254	300	286	367	355
Control*	M	S&L	S	S&L	S&L	S&L	S&L	S	S	S&L	M

Tuition and required fees (in dollars)	New York	North Carolina	North Dakota	Ohio	Okla-homa	Oregon	Pennsyl-vania	Rhode Island	South Carolina	South Dakota	Tennes-see
0	8										
1-99		13			1						
100-199		44		1	11				6		11
200-299				1	11	9	2		10		1
300-399	1		4	6	2	4	5	1	1		
400-499	8		1	9	1		9				
500-599	17			3		1			8		
600-699	10			9							
700-799	1			11			18				
800-899											
900-999											
1,000-1,099											
Number of institutions	45	57	5	40	15	14	34	1	25	0	12
Average tuition and required fees	455	120	350	546	252	301	624	300	318		188
Control*	S&L	S&L	M	M	M	S&L	M	S	M		S

(continued on next page)

Table 1 (*continued*)

Tuition and required fees (in dollars)	Texas	Utah	Vermont	Virginia	Washington	West Virginia	Wisconsin	Wyoming
0							37	
1-99	4							
100-199	44					1		
200-299	5			26	27	4		7
300-399	1	5				1		
400-499				1			12	
500-599								
600-699								
700-799			1					
800-899								
900-999								
1,000-1,099			1					
Number of institutions	54	5	2	27	27	6	49	7
Average tuition and required fees	145	330	860	233	244	253	112	252
Control*	S&L	S	S	M	S&L	S	M	S&L

*Control symbols: S, State; S&L, State and Local; M, Mixed; F, Federal.

Source: American Association of Community and Junior Colleges (1974).

Table 2. Average tuition and required fees in public two-year colleges
for district residents, 1972-73, by percentage of revenue from
local sources, by state, 1971-72

Average tuition and required fees (in dollars)	*Percentage of revenue from local sources*				
	0	*1-19*	*20-39*	*40-59*	*60 or more*
0					
1-99	1			1	1
100-199	1	3	3		1
200-299	7	1	5	1	1
300-399	7	3	4	1	
400-499		1	1		
500-599			1		
600-699			1		
700-799					
800-899					
Average tuition and required fees	266	242	351	218	62

Sources: American Association of Community and Junior Colleges (1974); and National Commission on the Financing of Postsecondary Education (1973, pp. 395-397).

Table 3. Average tuition and required fees in public two-year colleges
for district residents, 1972-73, and per capita personal income,
1972, by state

Average tuition and required fees (in dollars)	*Per capita personal income (in dollars)*				
	3,000- 3,499	*3,500- 3,999*	*4,000- 4,499*	*4,500- 4,999*	*5,000 and over*
0					
1-99			1	1	2
100-199	2	4	2		
200-299	1	4	8	1	3
300-399	1	5	4	4	2
400-499			1		1
500-599				1	

(continued on next page)

Table 3 *(continued)*

Average tuition and required fees (in dollars)	Per capita personal income (in dollars)				
	3,000-3,499	3,500-3,999	4,000-4,499	4,500-4,999	5,000 and over
600-699			1		
700-799					
800-899		1			
Average tuition and required fees	239	228	265	363	188

Sources: American Association of Community and Junior Colleges (1974); and U.S. Bureau of the Census (1973, p. 326).

Table 4. Average tuition and required fees in public two-year colleges for district residents, by percent of total enrollment in private institutions, by state, 1972-73

Average tuition and required fees (in dollars)	Percent of enrollment in private institutions					
	0-9	10-19	20-29	30-39	40-49	50 and over
0						
1-99	2	1	2			1
100-199	1	5	4			
200-299	1	10	4	1	1	
300-399	3	5		2	1	1
400-499			1	1	1	
500-599						
600-699					1	
700-799						
800-899					1	
Average tuition and required fees	201	179	286	342	514	323

Sources: American Association of Community and Junior Colleges (1974); and U.S. National Center for Educational Statistics (1974a, p. 68).

Table 5. Average tuition and required fees in public two-year colleges for district residents, by state and region, 1972-73

Average tuition and required fees (in dollars)	North-east	Middle Atlantic	East North Central	West North Central	South Atlantic	East South Central	West South Central	Mountain	Pacific
0									
1-99					1			1	2
100-199			1	1	1	2	3	1	
200-299	2		1	2	4	1	1	3	2
300-399	3	1	2	2	3	1		3	1
400-499		1		1					
500-599			1						
600-699		1							
700-799									
800-899	1								
Average tuition and required fees	314	502	297	311	223	231	166	229	85
Percent of total enrollment in private institutions	50	39	22	22	24	18	16	13	10

Source: American Association of Community and Junior Colleges (1974).

Table 6. Average tuition and required fees, public two-year colleges,
by state, 1968-69 and 1972-73

State	1968-69	1972-73	*Average annual rate of change*
Alabama	$180	$203	3.1%
Alaska	200	200	0
Arizona	0	48	
Arkansas	209	187	−2.7
California	0	2	
Colorado	153	232	11.0
Connecticut	100	229	23.0
Delaware	350	390	2.7
District of Columbia	90	90	0
Florida	165	244	10.3
Georgia	213	281	7.2
Hawaii	50	50	0
Idaho	170	298	15.1
Illinois	144	232	12.7
Indiana	435	365	−4.3
Iowa	318	410	6.6
Kansas	139	220	12.2
Kentucky	279	367	7.1
Louisiana	160	121	−6.7
Maine	247	340	8.3
Maryland	269	305	3.2
Massachusetts	246	337	8.2
Michigan	265	337	6.2
Minnesota	274	373	8.1
Mississippi	146	181	5.5
Missouri	180	241	7.6
Montana	175	185	1.4
Nebraska	154	254	13.3
Nevada	270	300	2.7
New Hampshire	300	286	−1.2

Table 6

State	1968-69	1972-73	*Average annual rate of change*
New Jersey	$290	$367	6.1%
New Mexico	347	355	0.6
New York	331	455	8.3
North Carolina	111	120	2.0
North Dakota	281	350	5.6
Ohio	469	546	3.9
Oklahoma	232	252	2.1
Oregon	219	301	8.3
Pennsylvania	451	624	8.5
Rhode Island	225	300	7.5
South Carolina	359	318	−3.0
Tennessee	165	188	3.3
Texas	105	145	8.4
Utah	264	330	5.7
Vermont	400	860	21.1
Virginia	179	233	6.8
Washington	210	244	3.8
West Virginia	218	253	3.8
Wisconsin	260	112	−19.0
Wyoming	160	252	12.0
United States	226	252	2.8

Source: Computed from data in American Association of Community and Junior Colleges (1969; 1974).

Note: South Dakota has no public two-year colleges.

Table 7. Frequency distribution of undergraduate tuition and required fees for state residents, public universities, by state, 1973-74

Tuition and required fees (in dollars)	United States	Alabama	Alaska	Arizona	Arkansas	California	Colorado	Connecticut	Delaware	District of Columbia	Florida
0	0										
1-99	0										
100-199	0										
200-299	1										
300-399	10			1							
400-499	24		1	1	1		1				
500-599	30	2					1		1		2
600-699	22					7	1				
700-799	9							1			
800-899	5										
900-999	4										
1,000-1,099	2										
Number of institutions	108*	2	1	2	1	7	3	1	1	0	2
Average tuition and required fees	576	518	472	366	400	637	527	715	525	—	570

*CUNY Graduate Center excluded

Tuition and required fees (in dollars)	Georgia	Hawaii	Idaho	Illinois	Indiana	Iowa	Kansas	Kentucky	Louisiana	Maine	Maryland
0											
1-99											
100-199											
200-299		1									
300-399			1						1		
400-499	1						1	1			
500-599	2			2			1			1	
600-699				2	2	2					1
700-799					1						
800-899											
900-999								1			
1,000-1,099											
Number of institutions	3	1	1	4	3	2	2	2	1	1	1
Average tuition and required fees	506	223	380	618	660	610	504	715	320	550	698

(continued on next page)

Table 7 (continued)

Tuition and required fees (in dollars)	Massachusetts	Michigan	Minnesota	Mississippi	Missouri	Montana	Nebraska	Nevada	New Hampshire	New Jersey	New Mexico
0											
1-99											
100-199											
200-299											
300-399											
400-499				1		2					2
500-599	1	1		2	3		1	1		1	
600-699		2	1								
700-799											
800-899		1									
900-999									1		
1,000-1,099											
Number of institutions	1	4	1	3	3	2	1	1	1	1	2
Average tuition and required fees	520	688	682	500	560	479	535	519	984	585	461

Tuition and required fees (in dollars)	New York	North Carolina	North Dakota	Ohio	Oklahoma	Oregon	Pennsylvania	Rhode Island	South Carolina	South Dakota	Tennessee
0											
1-99											
100-199											
200-299											
300-399											2
400-499		2	2		2						
500-599						2			1	1	
600-699									1		
700-799				6				1			
800-899	3			1			1				
900-999				1			1				
1,000-1,099							1				
Number of institutions	3	2	2	8	2	2	3	1	2	1	2
Average tuition and required fees	Division low up 750/ 900	457	446	789	447	519	958	761	605	556	374

(continued on next page)

Table 7 (*continued*)

Tuition and required fees (in dollars)	Texas	Utah	Vermont	Virginia	Washington	West Virginia	Wisconsin	Wyoming
0								
1-99								
100-199								
200-299	4							
300-399	3					1		
400-499		2						1
500-599				2	2			
600-699				1			2	
700-799								
800-899								
900-999								
1,000-1,099			1					
Number of institutions	7	2	1	3	2	1	2	1
Average tuition and required fees	299	467	1082	589	564	310	Division low up 573/ 628	430

Source: U.S. National Center for Educational Statistics (1974b).

Table 8. Average resident undergraduate tuition and required fees
in public universities, 1973-74, and per capita personal income,
1972, by state

Average tuition and required fees (in dollars)	*Per capita personal income (in dollars)*				
	3,000-3,499	*3,500-3,999*	*4,000-4,499*	*4,500-4,999*	*5,000-5,499*
0					
1-99					
100-199					
200-299			1	1	
300-399		4	1		
400-499	1	6	1		1
500-599	2	3	7	3	2
600-699	1		4	2	2
700-799		1	1	1	1
800-899					1
900-999			2		
1,000-1,099		1			
Average tuition and required fees	518	496	560	666	650

Sources: U.S. National Center for Educational Statistics (1974b); and U.S. Bureau of
the Census (1973, p. 326).

Table 9. Average resident undergraduate tuition and required fees
in public universities, by percent of total enrollment in
private institutions, by state, 1973-74

Average tuition and required fees (in dollars)	Percent of enrollment in private institutions					
	0-9	10-19	20-29	30-39	40-49	50 or more
0						
1-99						
100-199						
200-299	1	1				
300-399	1	3	1			
400-499	4	3	1	1		
500-599	1	10	5			1
600-699		4	4	1		
700-799		1	1	1	1	
800-899				1		
900-999					2	
1,000-1,099					1	
Average tuition and required fees	419	510	628	668	950	520

Sources: U.S. National Center for Educational Statistics (1974b); and "Opening Fall
Enrollments, 1972 and 1973" (1974).

Table 10. Average resident undergraduate tuition and required fees in public universities, by state and region, 1973-74

Average tuition and required fees (in dollars)	North-east	Middle Atlantic	East North Central	West North Central	South Atlantic	East South Central	West South Central	Mountain	Pacific
0									
1-99									
100-199									
200-299								1	1
300-399					1	1	1	2	
400-499				1	1		2	4	1
500-599	2	1		4	4	2		2	2
600-699			4	2	2				1
700-799	2		1			1			
800-899		1							
900-999	1	1							
1,000-1,099	1								
Average tuition and required fees	769	848	698	548	539	524	337	461	563
Percent of total enrollment in private institutions	49	38	21	22	24	17	16	13	10

Source: U.S. National Center for Educational Statistics (1974b).

Table 11. Frequency distribution of undergraduate tuition and required fees for state residents, public comprehensive universities and colleges, by state, 1973-74

Tuition and required fees (in dollars)	United States	Alabama	Alaska	Arizona	Arkansas	California	Colorado	Connecticut	Delaware	District of Columbia	Florida
0	0										
1-99	0										
100-199	24					16				1	
200-299	29						1				
300-399	56	2		1			2		1		
400-499	76	5			8		4	1			
500-599	64	3						3			5
600-699	20										
700-799	28										
800-899	6										
900-999											
1,000-1,099											
Number of institutions	304	10	0	1	8	16	7	4	1	1	5
Average tuition and required fees	459	455	—	330	404	160	399	519	345	132	570

Tuition and required fees (in dollars)	Georgia	Hawaii	Idaho	Illinois	Indiana	Iowa	Kansas	Ken-tucky	Louisi-ana	Maine	Mary-land
0											
1-99											
100-199											
200-299		1	1						5		
300-399	3		2				2		6		
400-499	9			1			1	5		3	
500-599				4			2				5
600-699				1	4	1					1
700-799											
800-899											
900-999											
1,000-1,099											
Number of institutions	12	1	3	6	4	1	5	5	11	3	6
Average tuition and required fees	414	228	325	561	629	600	474	424	308	417	564

(continued on next page)

Table 11 (*continued*)

Tuition and required fees (in dollars)	Massachusetts	Michigan	Minnesota	Mississippi	Missouri	Montana	Nebraska	Nevada	New Hampshire	New Jersey	New Mexico
0											
1-99											
100-199											
200-299					2						
300-399	7			2	5						2
400-499	3	2	5	3		3	2				1
500-599		8	1		1		2	1		4	
600-699			2				1			4	
700-799									2		
800-899											
900-999											
1,000-1,099											
Number of institutions	10	10	8	5	8	3	5	1	2	8	3
Average tuition and required fees	363	528	521	418	333	428	538	532	722	605	375

Tuition and required fees (in dollars)	New York	North Carolina	North Dakota	Ohio	Oklahoma	Oregon	Pennsylvania	Rhode Island	South Carolina	South Dakota	Tennessee
0											
1-99											
100-199	6										
200-299											
300-399		3			9						5
400-499		6	3						1		2
500-599		2		1		4		1	1	4	
600-699		1		2					1		
700-799	10			1			12			1	
800-899	1						4				
900-999											
1,000-1,099											
Number of institutions	17	12	3	4	9	4	16	1	3	5	7
Average tuition and required fees	CUNY 138 SUNY 762	464	407	672	355	523	768	490	560	579	369

(continued on next page)

Table 11 (continued)

Tuition and required fees (in dollars)	Texas	Utah	Vermont	Virginia	Washington	West Virginia	Wisconsin	Wyoming
0								
1-99								
100-199	1							
200-299	12					7		
300-399	2	1				1		
400-499		1		3	3	1		
500-599				1			11	
600-699				2				
700-799				2				
800-899			1					
900-999								
1,000-1,099				1				
Number of institutions	15	2	1	9	3	9	11	0
Average tuition and required fees	267	395	810	695	495	284	555	—

Source: U.S. National Center for Educational Statistics (1974b).

Table 12. Average resident undergraduate tuition and required fees
in public comprehensive universities and colleges, 1973-74,
and per capita personal income, 1972, by state

Average tuition and required fees (in dollars)	*Per capita personal income (in dollars)*				
	3,000- 3,499	*3,500- 3,999*	*4,000- 4,499*	*4,500- 4,999*	*5,000 or more*
0					
1-99					
100-199					2
200-299		1	1	1	
300-399		6	3	2	
400-499	3	6	2	1	
500-599	1	1	5	2	4
600-699			3	1	1
700-799			2		
800-899		1			
Average tuition and required fees	444	395	528	484	429

Note: Alaska and Wyoming have no institutions in this classification.

Sources: U.S. National Center for Educational Statistics (1974b); and U.S. Bureau of the Census (1973, p. 326).

Table 13. Average resident undergraduate tuition and required fees in public comprehensive universities and colleges, by percent of total enrollment in private institutions, by state, 1973-74

Average tuition and required fees (in dollars)	Percent of enrollment in private institutions					
	0-9	10-19	20-29	30-39	40-49	50 or more
0						
1-99						
100-199		1				1
200-299	1	2				
300-399	2	5	2	1		1
400-499	1	8	2		1	
500-599	1	5	5	2		
600-699		1	3	1		
700-799					2	
800-899					1	
Average tuition and required fees	382	406	506	528	752	342

Note: Alaska and Wyoming have no institutions in this classification.

Sources: U.S. National Center for Educational Statistics (1974b); and "Opening Fall Enrollments, 1972 and 1973" (1974).

Table 14. Average resident undergraduate tuition and required fees in public comprehensive universities and colleges, by state and region, 1973-74

Average tuition and required fees (in dollars)	North-east	Middle Atlantic	East North Central	West North Central	South Atlantic	East South Central	West South Central	Mountain	Pacific
0									
1-99									
100-199	1				1				1
200-299						1	1		1
300-399				1	2		2	5	
400-499	2			2	2	3	1	1	1
500-599	1	1	3	3	3			1	1
600-699		1	2	1	1				
700-799	1	1							
800-899	1								
Average tuition and required fees	462	642	570	474	478	420	322	391	265
Percent of total enrollment in private institutions	49	38	21	22	24	17	16	13	10

Source: U.S. National Center for Educational Statistics (1974b).

Low or No Tuition

Table 15. Appropriations for comprehensive state undergraduate
student aid programs, by state, 1974-75

State	Total appropriations (in dollars)	Total enrollment, fall 1974	Appropriations per enrolled student (dollars)
Alabama	—	144,185	—
Alaska	—	14,118	—
Arizona	—	152,218	—
Arkansas	—	56,674	—
California	41,057,114	1,530,178	26.83
Colorado	7,042,800	136,469	51.61
Connecticut	2,666,500	144,925	18.40
Delaware	75,000	29,053	2.58
District of Columbia	—	81,421	—
Florida	4,864,055	308,068	15.79
Georgia	1,186,116	155,643	7.62
Hawaii	35,000	43,861	0.80
Idaho	—	35,714	—
Illinois	63,220,000	533,249	118.56
Indiana	11,800,000	202,624	58.24
Iowa	6,572,591	113,719	57.80
Kansas	2,883,500	113,240	25.46
Kentucky	554,500	113,296	4.89
Louisiana	—	140,565	—
Maine	383,660	36,634	10.47
Maryland	320,500	186,604	1.72
Massachusetts	11,198,000	350,759	31.93
Michigan	18,567,928	452,570	41.03
Minnesota	8,526,365	166,196	51.30
Mississippi	—	86,945	—
Missouri	3,874,786	200,751	19.30
Montana	—	27,982	—
Nebraska	286,332	67,292	14.26
Nevada	—	24,768	—
New Hampshire	—	34,399	—

Table 15

State	Total appropriations (in dollars)	Total enrollment, fall 1974	Appropriations per enrolled student (dollars)
New Jersey	27,579,250	274,313	100.54
New Mexico	–	50,666	–
New York	108,450,000	954,471	113.62
North Carolina	–	223,172	–
North Dakota	255,500	28,544	8.95
Ohio	17,540,000	408,345	42.95
Oklahoma	540,000	132,802	4.07
Oregon	2,333,853	138,545	16.85
Pennsylvania	73,191,262	446,799	163.81
Rhode Island	1,983,650	59,436	33.37
South Carolina	6,080,000	114,402	53.15
South Dakota	212,620	26,855	7.92
Tennessee	3,618,205	163,887	22.08
Texas	7,500,000	548,829	13.67
Utah	–	84,760	–
Vermont	2,804,000	28,289	99.12
Virginia	800,000	214,965	3.72
Washington	3,195,972	210,013	15.22
West Virginia	1,500,000	71,250	21.05
Wisconsin	13,668,500	227,235	60.15
Wyoming	–	16,132	–
U.S.	456,367,559	10,107,830	45.15
Service Schools	–	29,235	–
U.S. including Service Schools		10,137,065	45.02

Sources: Scholarship appropriations data from Winkler (1974, p. 6); enrollment data from "Opening Fall Enrollments, 1972, 1973, and 1974" (1974).

Table 16. Appropriations for comprehensive state undergraduate student aid programs per enrolled student, by percent of total enrollment in private institutions, by state, 1974-75

Appropriations per student (in dollars)	Percent of enrollment in private institutions					
	0-9	10-19	20-29	30-39	40-49	50 and over
0	5	5	2	1	1	1
1-9	2	6	2			
10-19		4	2	1		
20-29		3	1			
30-39					1	1
40-49		1	1			
50-59		1	3	1		
60-69		1				
70-79						
80-89						
90-99					1	
100-119			2		1	
120-139						
140-159						
160-179					1	
Average	$3.91	$21.11	$58.34	$26.90	$122.38	$25.91

Sources: Computed from data in Table 15 and in "Opening Fall Enrollments, 1972, 1973, and 1974" (1974).

Table 17. Expenditures of state and local governments on higher education
as percentage of state personal income, by percentage of total
state enrollment in private institutions, 1972

Expenditures as percentage of personal income	Percentage of total state enrollment in private institutions					
	0-9	10-19	20-29	30-39	40-49	50 and over
0 to 0.49						
0.50 to 0.69			1	2	1	1
0.70 to 0.89	1	4	4		1	
0.90 to 1.09	1	9	5	1	2	
1.10 to 1.29	2	3	2		1	
1.30 to 1.49	2	4		1		
1.50 and over	1	1				
Average*	1.22	1.11	0.96	0.95	0.90	0.60

*Unweighted average of state percentages.

Sources: U.S. Bureau of the Census (1973, p. 326); U.S. National Center for Educational Statistics (1974a, p. 68); and unpublished NCES data.

Table 18. Amount each state would receive under an illustrative formula for federal grants to states (millions of dollars)

State	Percent of population aged 18 to 34, 1973	Percent of undergrad FTE enroll-ment, 1971	Population allocation	FTE allocation	Total, unadjusted	Total, adjusted for per capita income factor*
United States	100.00	100.00	$1,000.00	$1,000.00	$2,000.00	$2,000.00
Alabama	1.63	1.42	16.3	14.2	30.5	34.4
Alaska	0.19	0.08	1.9	0.8	2.7	2.5
Arizona	0.97	1.18	9.7	11.8	21.5	21.9
Arkansas	0.90	0.73	9.0	7.3	16.3	18.3
California	10.27	12.71	102.7	127.1	229.8	216.4
Colorado	1.29	1.47	12.9	14.7	27.6	27.7
Connecticut	1.39	1.36	13.9	13.6	27.5	24.8
Delaware	0.28	0.29	2.8	2.9	5.7	5.4
District of Columbia	0.41	0.61	4.1	6.1	10.2	8.0
Florida	3.20	2.91	32.0	29.1	61.1	63.1
Georgia	2.40	1.65	24.0	16.5	40.5	43.4
Hawaii	0.44	0.45	4.4	4.5	8.9	8.4
Idaho	0.36	0.47	3.6	4.7	8.3	9.1
Illinois	5.18	5.00	51.8	50.0	101.8	94.4
Indiana	2.52	2.31	25.2	23.1	48.3	48.8

Iowa	1.29	1.44	12.9	14.4	27.3	27.8
Kansas	1.07	1.32	10.7	13.2	23.9	23.6
Kentucky	1.57	1.26	15.7	12.6	28.3	31.1
Louisiana	1.78	1.61	17.8	16.1	33.9	37.5
Maine	0.45	0.42	4.5	4.2	8.7	9.6
Maryland	1.99	1.56	19.9	15.6	35.5	33.8
Massachusetts	3.26	3.39	32.6	33.9	66.5	63.6
Michigan	4.29	4.37	42.9	43.7	86.6	83.3
Minnesota	1.86	1.89	18.6	18.9	37.5	38.1
Mississippi	1.04	1.02	10.4	10.2	20.6	23.9
Missouri	2.16	2.11	21.6	21.1	42.7	44.0
Montana	0.33	0.40	3.3	4.0	7.3	7.8
Nebraska	0.71	0.82	7.1	8.2	15.3	15.5
Nevada	0.26	0.16	2.6	1.6	4.2	3.9
New Hampshire	0.37	0.40	3.7	4.0	7.7	8.0
New Jersey	3.17	2.33	31.7	23.3	55.0	51.0
New Mexico	0.53	0.53	5.3	5.3	10.6	11.6
New York	8.28	8.83	82.8	88.3	171.1	155.0
North Carolina	2.63	2.44	26.3	24.4	50.7	55.0
North Dakota	0.29	0.42	2.9	4.2	7.1	7.7
Ohio	4.98	4.70	49.8	47.0	96.8	96.4
Oklahoma	1.23	1.43	12.3	14.3	26.6	28.6
Oregon	1.93	1.40	19.3	14.0	33.3	34.0

(continued on next page)

Table 18 (continued)

State	Percent of population aged 18 to 34, 1973	Percent of undergrad FTE enrollment, 1971	Population allocation	FTE allocation	Total, unadjusted	Total, adjusted for per capita income factor*
Pennsylvania	5.11	4.76	51.1	47.6	98.7	99.0
Rhode Island	0.46	0.52	4.6	5.2	9.8	9.9
South Carolina	1.38	1.03	13.8	10.3	24.1	26.9
South Dakota	0.30	0.40	3.0	4.0	7.0	7.6
Tennessee	1.98	1.79	19.8	17.9	37.7	41.2
Texas	5.76	5.42	57.6	54.2	111.8	117.2
Utah	0.59	1.06	5.9	10.6	16.5	17.9
Vermont	0.23	0.31	2.3	3.1	5.4	5.8
Virginia	2.52	1.76	25.2	17.6	42.8	43.9
Washington	1.69	2.17	16.9	21.7	38.6	38.6
West Virginia	0.78	0.84	7.8	8.4	16.2	17.8
Wisconsin	2.13	2.56	21.3	25.6	46.9	48.3
Wyoming	0.17	0.21	1.7	2.1	3.8	3.9

*State allocation adjusted upward by one-half of the difference between the ratio of its 1972 per capita income to the national average and 1.00, if below national average, and adjusted downward by corresponding amount if above national average. For example, a state with a ratio of 0.80 would receive 110 percent of its unadjusted amount, while a state with a ratio of 1.20 would receive 90 percent of its unadjusted amount.

References

American Association of Community and Junior Colleges. *Directory, 1969.* Washington, D.C., 1969.

American Association of Community and Junior Colleges. *Directory, 1974.* Washington, D.C., 1974.

American Council on Education. *Higher Education and National Affairs,* Feb. 15, 1974, *23.*

Association of American Colleges. *A National Policy for Private Higher Education.* The Report of a Task Force of the National Council of Independent Colleges and Universities. Washington, D.C., 1974.

Bowen, H. R. *Financing Higher Education: The Current State of the Debate.* Washington, D.C.: Association of American Colleges, 1974.

Carnegie Commission on Higher Education. *The Open-Door Colleges: Policies for Community Colleges.* New York: McGraw-Hill, 1970.

Carnegie Commission on Higher Education. *The Capitol and the Campus: State Responsibility for Postsecondary Education.* New York: McGraw-Hill, 1971.

Carnegie Commission on Higher Education. *Institutional Aid: Federal Support to Colleges and Universities.* New York: McGraw-Hill, 1972.

Carnegie Commission on Higher Education. *A Classification of Institutions of Higher Education.* Berkeley, Calif., 1973a.

Carnegie Commission on Higher Education. *Higher Education: Who Pays? Who Benefits? Who Should Pay?* New York: McGraw-Hill, 1973b.

Carnegie Commission on Higher Education. *Tuition: A Supplemental Statement to the Report of the Carnegie Commission on Higher Education on 'Who Pays? Who Benefits? Who Should Pay?'* Berkeley, Calif., 1974.

Conant, J. B. *My Several Lives: Memoirs of a Social Inventor.* New York: Harper and Row, 1970.

"Cutting Tuition in Half: Wisconsin Plan Under Political Attack." *Chronicle of Higher Education,* Oct. 29, 1974, p. 7.

Education Commission of the States. *Higher Education in the States,* vol. 2, no. 6. Denver, Colo., 1971.

Education Commission of the States. Unpublished tables on state scholarship programs and aid to private institutions. Denver, Colo., 1974.

Fried, E. R., et al. *Setting National Priorities: The 1974 Budget.* Washington, D.C.: The Brookings Institution, 1973.

Gordon, M. S. *Statement Prepared for the Special Subcommittee on Education,* U.S. House of Representatives, June 25, 1974.

Hansen, W. L., and Weisbrod, B. A. *A New Approach to Higher Education Finance.* University of Wisconsin: Institute for Research on Poverty, Discussion Papers, 1970.

Kirschling, W., and Postweiler, R. *General Institutional Assistance: A Scheme that Depends on the Educational Efforts of the States and the Attendance Choice of Students.* Boulder, Colo.: Western Interstate Commission for Higher Education, 1971.

Kirschling, W., and Postweiler, R. *A Proposal for General Federal Assistance to Postsecondary Education: The Kirschling-Postweiler Plan.* Unpublished paper, Western Interstate Commission for Higher Education. Boulder, Colo., 1974.

Millard, R. M. "State Aid to Nonpublic Higher Education." In Education Commission of the States, *Higher Education in the States,* vol. 4, no. 5. Denver, Colo., 1974.

National Commission on the Financing of Postsecondary Education. *Financing Postsecondary Education in the United States.* Washington, D.C., 1973.

Nerlove, M. "On Tuition and the Costs of Higher Education: Prolegomena to a Conceptual Framework." *Journal of Political Economy,* May-June 1972, *80,* S178-S218.

"Opening Fall Enrollments, 1972 and 1973." *Chronicle of Higher Education,* Jan. 14, 1974, p. 10.

"Opening Fall Enrollments, 1972, 1973, and 1974." *Chronicle of Higher Education,* Dec. 16, 1974, p. 8.

The President's Commission on Higher Education. *Higher Education for American Democracy.* 6 vols. Washington, D.C., 1947.

Suchar, E. W., Van Dusen, W. D., and Jacobson, E. C. *Student Expenses at Postsecondary Institutions, 1974-75.* New York: College Entrance Examination Board, 1974.

Tirrell, J. E., and McGuinness, A. *A Proposal for a New Title IV.* Statement Prepared for the Special Subcommittee on Education, Committee on Education and Labor, U.S. House of Representatives. Washington, D.C., July 15, 1974.

U.S. Bureau of the Census. *Statistical Abstract of the United States, 1973.* Washington, D.C., 1973.

U.S. National Center for Educational Statistics. *Digest of Educational Statistics, 1972.* Washington, D.C., 1973.

U.S. National Center for Educational Statistics. *Digest of Educational Statistics, 1973.* Washington, D.C., 1974a.

U.S. National Center for Educational Statistics. *Education Directory, 1973-74: Higher Education.* Washington, D.C., 1974b.

U.S. National Center for Educational Statistics. *Projections of Educational Statistics to 1982-83, 1973 Edition.* Washington, D.C., 1974c.

University of Wisconsin System. *1975 to 1977 Biennial Operating Budget Policy Paper #2.0: Statement of Major Biennial Policy Issues and Contributing Problems.* Madison, Wis., September 1974. (Duplicated.)

Wattenbarger, J. L., and Sakaguchi, M. *State Level Boards for Community Junior Colleges: Patterns of Control and Coordination.* Gainesville, Fla.: Institute of Higher Education, University of Florida, 1971.

Winkler, K. J. "States Raise Aid to Students 25 Pct." *Chronicle of Higher Education,* Nov. 18, 1974, pp. 1, 6.

Index